GLOBAL
TILT

GLOBAL TILT

LEADING YOUR BUSINESS THROUGH THE GREAT ECONOMIC POWER SHIFT

RAM CHARAN
With Geri Willigan
and Charles Burck

CROWN
BUSINESS
NEW YORK

Copyright © 2013 by Ram Charan

Published in the United States by Crown Business, an imprint of the Crown
Publishing Group, a division of Random House, Inc., New York.

www.crownpublishing.com

CROWN BUSINESS is a trademark and CROWN and the Rising Sun
colophon are registered trademarks of Random House, Inc.

Crown Business books are available at special discounts for bulk purchases
for sales promotions or corporate use. Special editions, including personalized
covers, excerpts of existing books, or books with corporate logos, can be created
in large quantities for special needs. For more information, contact Premium
Sales at (212) 572-2232 or e-mail specialmarkets@randomhouse.com.

Library of Congress Cataloging-in-Publication Data

Charan, Ram, author.
Global tilt: leading your business through the great economic power shift /
Ram Charan.—First Edition.
pages   cm
Includes bibliographical references and index.
1. Economic development—Developing countries. 2. International
cooperation. 3. Leadership—Developing countries. 4. Organizational change.
I. Title.

HD82.C4623 2013

338.9009172'4—dc23

2012033678

ISBN 978-0-307-88912-6
eISBN 978-0-307-88914-0
Printed in the United States of America

Book design by Maria Elias

1   3   5   7   9   10   8   6   4   2

First Edition

Dedicated to the hearts and souls of the joint family of twelve siblings and cousins living under one roof for fifty years, whose personal sacrifices made my formal education possible

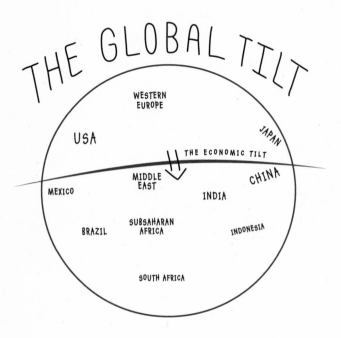

THE GLOBAL TILT

WESTERN
EUROPE

USA   JAPAN

                            THE ECONOMIC TILT
            MIDDLE
            EAST   CHINA
MEXICO
                        INDIA

            SUBSAHARAN
BRAZIL   AFRICA   INDONESIA

            SOUTH AFRICA

GLOBAL TILT:

A DEFINITION

global tilt ('glō-bəl tilt) 1. The shift in business and economic power from countries of the North to those below the thirty-first parallel; 2. the greatest change in business history; 3. a call for leaders to abandon old mindsets, rules of thumb, and assumptions about the North and South and the relationship between the two; 4. the result of unstoppable forces, including the unleashed energies of the South, demographic shifts, the volatile global financial system, and digitization; 5. the opening of megaopportunities for those who can handle complexity, speed, volatility, and uncertainty; 6. the spur to radical changes in strategic thinking, leadership, and the organization's social system.

CONTENTS

PART I

WELCOME TO THE TILTED WORLD

CHAPTER ONE

CHANGE YOU CAN'T IGNORE

3

CHAPTER TWO

WHAT YOU NEED TO
KNOW FIRST

25

CHAPTER THREE

THE NEW POWER OF THE SOUTH

97

PART II

HOW TO SUCCEED IN THE GLOBAL TILT

CHAPTER FOUR

OUTSIDE IN & FUTURE BACK:
STRATEGY FOR A TILTED WORLD

153

CHAPTER FIVE

MASTERING MULTIPLE CONTEXTS:
LEADERSHIP IN A TILTED WORLD

185

CHAPTER SIX

SHIFTING POWER, RESOURCES, AND BEHAVIOR:
THE ORGANIZATION IN A TILTED WORLD

219

CHAPTER SEVEN

NORTH COMPANIES AT THE FRONT:
MAKING BETS ON MARKET GROWTH

255

YOUR GLOBAL FUTURE
295

ACKNOWLEDGMENTS

305

NOTES

309

INDEX

315

PART I

WELCOME TO THE
TILTED WORLD

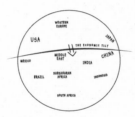

CHAPTER ONE

CHANGE YOU CAN'T IGNORE

L ate on November 24, 2010, I landed in Dubai, where I would be speaking at a corporate meeting for India's number one telecom company, Bharti Airtel. I had left New York twelve hours earlier, after three days of appointments with companies along the east coast of the United States. Some of the problems and questions I'd heard that week were still on my mind. The CEOs and senior and midlevel managers alike were wrestling with how the fallout from the debacle in Europe would affect their businesses. How deep and how long would the recession be? Like everyone, they felt battered by the headwinds of a slowing global economy, global competition, and fast change.

Arriving at the hotel, I freshened up and headed to the conference room, passing through the lobby, where 160 of Bharti's top managers were mingling. Forty-six of them were Africans who were new to the company following

Bharti's acquisition just a few months before of Zain, a collection of telecom assets in fifteen African countries. They were now part of the managerial mix of Bharti Airtel, along with leaders from Sri Lanka and Bangladesh, where the company had expanded the year before. Many wore typical Western business garb; others wore traditional African clothing. All were speaking English. The majority appeared to be in their thirties, and some looked even younger than that.

But youth alone didn't explain the unmistakable difference between this group and the leaders I'd seen just hours earlier—a physical and psychological ocean away. There was energy, optimism, and excitement in the air. This company, already among the top five mobile operators in the world in terms of subscribers, was on the move, and its leaders knew it. Bharti had grown from nothing to a multibillion-dollar global leader of its industry in a matter of fifteen years. *Why won't it win in the United States or Europe at some future point in time?* I wondered. Yet its phenomenal growth and the entrepreneurial verve of its founder, Sunil Mittal, are all but unknown in the northern hemisphere.

That moment crystallized for me an unmistakable truth: The world has tilted. Its economic center has shifted from what have traditionally been called the advanced or Western countries of the northern hemisphere to fast-developing countries including China, India, Indonesia, Brazil, and others in the Middle East and even parts of Africa. For decades the standard view was that the transfer of technology, managerial know-how, and capital was from West to East, from the United States and Western Europe to Japan, South Korea, and the Asian tigers. But today the flows are generally from North to South. In geographic terms, the dividing line is the thirty-first parallel. The division is rough—for example, Japan and South Korea are essentially Northern countries in their economies and business practices—but it's a simple shorthand way to view the tilt.

Wealth is moving from North to South, and so are jobs. Companies in the South, big and small, have a fierce entrepreneurial drive. Many are reveling in double-digit revenue growth, bringing jobs and prosperity to their home countries. They are building scale and challenging companies of the North on all fronts. They have huge momentum, while the old heavyweights—some of which have dominated their industries for decades—can barely eke out low to middle single-digit growth. The South is driving change. The North is afraid of it.

Many business leaders in the North are blind to the magnitude of trends. Some are accelerating the tilt by transferring their technology, brands, know-how, and real assets to the South, all in the search for much higher growth than they see in their own home base. Some blame such things as cheap labor, currency manipulation, and protectionism for their struggles. These are problems, but much bigger forces drive the tilt—and the Northern leaders have not yet come to terms with the world as it is today and as it is emerging. How, then, can they devise a clearheaded response? Understanding the new dynamics of global competition and economic behaviors is an unconditional requirement for business leaders from the North and the South, even in companies that are smaller or consider themselves domestic. Very few businesses are immune to the changes.

When we cut through the complexity and volatility, several unmistakable realities shine through.

The world is in an inevitable transition to a more even distribution of opportunity and wealth. It is fueled by an irrepressible and fundamental human drive: people's desire for a better life. While the road ahead will have unexpected twists and turns, its direction is clear, and we are moving at high speed.

The global financial system, which connects the economies of all countries every second of the day, is highly unstable. No one truly understands how it works, as evidenced by the seemingly unending ugly discoveries about the behavior of major players in the system. Its malfunctioning can cause recessions and damage entire economies, as it did in the 1997 economic "Asian Contagion" and the far more widespread loss of economic growth between 2007 and 2012. Uncertainty will continue to be the order of the day for some time to come.

We are in a war for jobs. Although total employment will continue to increase worldwide, every country is seeking a larger share of the jobs pie to create or strengthen its middle class, improve its standard of living, increase its financial reserves, and ensure political stability. Nationalism is alive and well as countries compete with no clear agreement about the rules of the game.

Many countries below the thirty-first parallel are creating their own rules of the road and executing their growth plans to win jobs and resources for their people. They are participating in the global economy without necessarily following the free-market principles of the North. China, Singapore, and Taiwan have explicit national economic strategies. Other countries, including Brazil and India, are beginning to shape their own. Protectionist policies are widespread; governments don't hesitate to step in on behalf of their countries' self-interest. The United States practices some protectionism in selected areas but has no coordinated economic plan.

Companies are competing against countries—not just other companies. When a government decides to back a domestic company, whether to protect its home base or to help it achieve world dominance, the competitive equation can shift drastically. State-sponsored companies can scale up quickly and often don't have the same profit requirements as their publicly traded competitors. Thus they can lower prices and reduce returns for an entire industry. What's more, the unwritten rule of global expansion is that the company putting down roots in the growth market will transfer its technology and managerial know-how to its native partners. That technology transfer can happen surprisingly quickly.

Northern companies may be building their future competition in exchange for access to markets. For example, in 2007 China set its sights on building an aircraft business that would compete globally. It welcomed U.S. and European aircraft makers to build plants in China, but stipulated that any foreign direct investment had to be through joint ventures with domestic companies. Such supplier relationships involve the open exchange of information, by which proprietary knowledge, accumulated over a long period and funded by taxpayer money and risk funds, can flow. Now Commercial Aircraft Corporation of China (COMAC) is gearing up to compete head-on against Boeing and Airbus with a homegrown narrow-body plane set for release in 2016.

India has the same kind of protections through ownership restrictions. In some industries, non-Indian companies are allowed to expand only if they give Indian firms an ownership stake. In defense-related businesses, including nuclear, the requirement is stiffer: Non-Indian companies are welcome only if they allow Indians to hold the majority stake.

Why are Northern companies willing to accept conditions dictated by the host country? Because they see the country as important to their current and future ability to deliver growth and shareholder value. Besides, they recognize that if they don't do it, a competitor will. But while individual managements make these decisions autonomously, their collective actions can affect their home country. When many companies shift their resources and attention to the same country in a short period of time in a herd effect, the home country suffers. Its unemployment increases, its tax base drops, its ratings decline, and both its budget and its trade deficits increase. Thus the collective pursuit of shareholder value, concentrated in one or two countries in the South that do not play by the rules of the game, can unwittingly undermine the national prosperity of their home country. One only has to think about the decline in recent decades of manufacturing in the United States to see the point.

Many companies of the South are tapping into the global supply of capital, know-how, and technology. They are on the offensive, paying top dollar for the best talent they can get from anywhere, often from the North. The McKinseys, Accentures, and IBMs of the world help would-be clients anywhere in the world. So do headhunters: Former executives of Fortune 500 companies are eager to lend their expertise to enterprises that are growing, and they are getting compensated on a U.S. pay scale. Indian outsourcing firm Wipro hired a former GE executive as its vice chairman (and effectively the chief operating officer for its founder), at an American level of compensation, to help build that business. Wipro then moved from a low ranking to being the number three India-based company in the world. Ever-expanding stock markets, private equity, sovereign wealth funds (investment money held by governments), and global banks are pouring money into opportunities wherever they find them; opportunity is of course defined by growth.

Like consultants, firms with special technological expertise will court customers wherever they can find them. Even after the formation of OPEC in 1973 and the gradual shift of power in negotiations thereafter, the major oil companies of the North had a lot of clout because of their size and proprietary know-how. But other industry players, such as Schlumberger, the world's leading independent oil-drilling specialist, sell their services and voluminous knowledge base to Saudi Arabia, Russia, Mexico, and others.

As economic power shifts, political power does too. In both, U.S. influence in the South is seen to be in decline, enabling some countries whose support America took for granted to go their own way. For example, against the wishes of the United States, Brazil refused to support sanctions aimed at deterring Iran's nuclear ambitions, a surprising political stance that would have been unimaginable five years earlier. Some African countries have shown a preference for dealing with China over America because America pushes a democratic ideology, while the Chinese do not. The one that has the money has the power. The one that holds the promise of tremendous economic growth opportunities has even more power. Economic power creates political power, not the other way around.

The tilt will seesaw along the way. Fortunes rise and fall; events that affect one country ripple through others. For example, the post-crisis woes of the European financial system that brought Europe's growth rate close to zero also slowed exports from the United States and China. The result has been more downward pressure on the U.S. economy and a significant deceleration in China's growth rate. Economic factors such as inflation rates are likely to dampen the comparative advantage China and many other Southern countries now have in wages and currencies against the North. It has already begun in parts of some industries.

Nonetheless, the overall direction of the tilt remains the same. Even after wage differentials narrow, the South will still have cost advantages. Over time, the tilt will persistently and inevitably continue to change the economic landscape, reshaping competitive dynamics and industry structures around the globe.

Like it or not, you have no choice but to figure out how to position your business in light of the changes. Sitting like the proverbial pigeon with its eyes closed hoping the cat won't see it is not a good plan. Waiting for protection from the government is not a good plan either. The wheels of democracy turn more slowly than the central planning used successfully elsewhere. Nor is it wise to go forward using the rearview mirror as a guide, comparing China and India with Japan's rise in earlier decades, for instance, as some business leaders and academics are known to do. Such comparisons are deeply flawed. Today's competitors are not following Northern models and seeking acceptance by the established international business community. This is a new century and a new game being played on an uneven playing field.

A CALL TO ACTION FOR
THE NORTH

If you're a leader in a North company, you have a narrow window of time in which to make a decisive tilt in your approach to running the business. You cannot rely on traditional approaches to competitive analysis, strategy, and execution. Your leadership must start with a clear grasp of the global context. While the North is suffering from low or no growth, the South is on the move, even now as the global economy cools. Projections with a long enough time horizon, say ten and twenty years out, capture the steepness of the growth curve of the South and the enormity of the opportunity. Companies that miss the window may permanently lose the chance to gain footing in the South, and at the same time, they make themselves vulnerable to attack on their home turf sometime down the road.

You can't dwell on whether the help that Southern companies are getting from their governments is "unfair." Life is unfair. Once you drop your defensive psychology and grasp the shift in economic gravity, the lightbulb will go on: How then do we pursue these opportunities fast enough and without losing sight of our home markets, which after all are still huge in absolute terms and attractive to competitors from the South? The answer lies in fundamental changes in how you think about strategy, as well as changes in power, resource allocation, and decision making, and in your personal development as a leader.

Opportunities in the North won't disappear, but companies that remain only in the North will struggle to find growth. Small moves into foreign markets designed to test the waters are not sufficient to meet the dynamism of South-based competitors. More and more, when the time and opportunity are right, you will face decisions about whether to make a big strategic bet or become entrepreneurial on a mega scale, as heavy hitters in the South do. In either case, you'll need a bigger appetite for risk than many Northern CEOs and their boards are accustomed to, and you might have to consider new kinds of partnerships to scale up quickly.

The simultaneous growth of many nations' economies is making "large scale" larger than ever, and the South is achieving it astonishingly fast. The barriers to entry that large companies of the North created are in many cases now broken. Young companies in the South, helped by American, Japanese, and German experts, are now capable of competing head-on with North-based giants. Singapore has become a financial center of Southeast Asia, Taiwan has become a dominant player in semiconductors, and Brazil is competing successfully in regional jets. Brazil's Vale rode the wave of China's surging demand to become the world's largest producer of iron ore. The Chinese government has been known to push consolidation among domestic competitors precisely to achieve scale, as it is doing in autos and tried to do in rare earth minerals.

South-based competitors have all the capital they need for their fast expansion. Some have government funding in the form of low-cost loans; others are using their country's sovereign wealth funds. Private equity firms are trolling for opportunities, and so are traditional investors, including those in the expanding stock markets of the South. A Southern company that shows it is on a growth trajectory gets rewarded with price-earnings ratios much higher than its peers in the North. Colgate, a Northern company with a strong presence in India, has a PE of 17 in the North, but its Indian division, which is listed separately on the Indian stock exchange, has a PE of 25.

Competing in the South means reckoning with the reality that the financial premiums you've long enjoyed may be at risk. Many upstarts there thrive on low margins, lowering profitability for the entire industry and throwing business models and financial expectations into question. Are you willing to forgo profits in the early years to win in the South? And can you convince the capital markets to live with a longer time horizon?

Explosive growth puts pressure on resources, including inputs that may be critical to your business. Some big players in the South, with the help of their governments, are making long-term deals to secure them. You might have to plan alternative suppliers of materials, alternative inputs, and alternative sources of energy, and even consider the possibility of vertical integration.

If you decide to grow aggressively in the South, you'll need some leaders who can navigate in those very different parts of the world and others who can keep the North motivated and renew growth in so-called mature markets. Importantly, you will need leaders who see the world not just from the vantage point of New York but also from that of Beijing, Mumbai, or Buenos Aires. One mistake is the common practice of sending envoys to countries for five-day visits and assuming you understand the market—you'll be deluding yourself. Another is to force local market intelligence through filters of a bureaucratic hierarchy that pays scant attention to the South, because it represents only a small percentage of current revenues. Decision making has to be close to the markets, and the markets must be segmented.

To begin with, you need to understand that the South has its own economic ecosystem, one that is only partly defined by its relationships with the North. Trade between its countries is exploding. China's ambitions may scare its neighbors, but its exports to the rest of the South continue to grow, and it is seeking to capture resources within the region. India is moving aggressively into Bangladesh,

Vietnam, Myanmar—whose ancient roots in Buddhism create a natural affinity—and countries of Africa. Its familiarity with poor infrastructure and governance gives it an advantage in dealing with these nations. And of course, Latin America has a longstanding history of trade within its region. Rolling all Southern countries into one lump designated as "emerging markets" makes you vulnerable to being outmaneuvered by local competitors and savvy global players who have already occupied key spaces. You've got to be on the spot to understand these dynamics. Real decision-making authority must shift, or tilt, to the South, along with funding. Any leaders you assign or hire locally must be high-level, so you're comfortable entrusting them with big decisions and hefty budgets.

Expansion requires commitment of people and money. In practical terms, that means extracting some of each from the North to build growth in the South. This is what stops many leaders in their tracks: they don't want to deal with people who are naturally concerned about losing their sphere of influence or even their jobs. Yet incremental shifts will almost certainly inhibit growth. Taking advantage of the tilt's growth opportunities requires leaving your comfort zone and getting the timing and direction of those organizational shifts right.

DISSECTING THE TILT

Leaders who have succeeded by understanding the granular details of their industries and immediate competitors now must master a new skill: understanding and anticipating the global business context. You need to develop your own perspective to detect trends that cut across not just industries but also countries, sometimes challenging the economic and business principles you're familiar with, and see how those trends stretch and bend as companies and countries act and react to one another. The better you are at this, the greater your competitive advantage will be.

You also have to be on the alert for single events that could be pivotal. Given the speed with which a single player can amass resources or a government can change the competitive ground rules, you must develop your skill in imagining second- and third-order consequences. This is where one astute leader can see a bend in the road ahead of time while others miss it.

Leaders from the South may have an advantage here because of the fast and multifaceted changes they've had to live with, but Northern leaders can learn this skill too. It's a matter of expanding the lens through which you see the world and applying both your intellect and your intuition to cut through to the essentials. And you can't delegate it to consultants or other experts, who will have their own points of view. Their input is useful, maybe even necessary, but you must build your own competence in doing it, because your view of the world will inform your actions and decisions.

There's no excuse for geoeconomic or geopolitical illiteracy. Information is readily available. Time for reflection is what's usually in short supply. You have to work at gaining command of trends beyond your industry and geography. Take, for instance, trade patterns. Whether China continues to build its trade surplus depends on several things: its ability to maintain its advantages in currency valuation and labor costs or increase domestic consumption, and other countries' reluctance to take defensive protectionist measures. Your conclusion may depend on your assessment of those factors.

Among the trends to watch is the changing role of government in economic activity. Will the United States become more effective in furthering its economic interests, and China less so? Will countries cooperate on common issues such as financial reform? Will new mechanisms emerge to resolve trade disputes?

You can't ignore the global financial system either. However hard it is to understand, you have to be able to identify for yourself the weak spots and early warning signals of a break point. (No one believes we've left the dark woods of systemic risk behind.) You don't have to be a governor of the Federal Reserve, but you must master the basics.

Your viewpoint about the world will give you a better sense of how to filter the sources of information you rely on, focus the business, allocate resources, select people, and organize their efforts. It will also change the way you allot your own time and mental energy.

THE ROCKY ROAD TO A MORE EQUAL WORLD

We are headed toward an expansion of wealth and opportunity to millions of people worldwide who are being lifted out of poverty into a burgeoning middle class. The gap between wealthy nations and poor ones is clearly narrowing by several measures. One is what populations can afford to buy in their home markets (what economists call purchasing power parity). Another is education: Consider the increase in the number of graduates with technical degrees, supplemented by technology centers Northern companies such as GE, Honeywell, and Siemens have been building in the past decade. It will take longer for the internal infrastructure, distribution channels, health care, and capital markets of the South to reach parity with the North, but they are well on their way.

While the notion of parity is universally appealing in

human terms, the transition will be challenging. Already we see the tug-of-war for resources and jobs played out through countries' willingness to practice their own versions of capitalism and free trade with varying degrees of protectionism. Trade imbalances are multiplying in number and size. When the Southern countries were still emerging, they typically ran deficits with developed countries of the North. Today the mix of surpluses and deficits is not so neatly partitioned. Taking into account both manufactured goods and services, in 2011 Germany and China enjoyed ample trade surpluses ($100.8 billion and $182.6 billion, respectively, as of June 2010). The United States, Britain, and India ran hefty trade deficits ($600 billion, $61 billion, and $145 billion).[1]

Why does such macro data matter to anybody but economists? Because it can affect your own business in the South. For example, India's growing deficit with China is at the point where it could do long-term damage as the rupee continues to decline. Many Indian companies that borrowed in hard currencies in recent years will have trouble repaying their debts; North companies doing business in India will need to make sure that their customers aren't at risk.

Economic shifts of such seismic scale occur only occasionally in human history. The last one took place over several centuries, beginning with the European Renaissance, when China, India, and Japan were the world's most powerful economies. This one developed in just a few decades. It got under way when Deng Xiaoping took power in China some three decades ago, but it greatly accelerated in the mid-1990s, when he implemented reforms that transformed China to a so-called socialist market economy. When that decade began, America was the world's dominant economic, technological, and political power. Ten years later it was a faltering giant. Financial innovations and a flood of money were fueling high consumption. China and other Southern countries provided the goods, and the United States amassed its towering trade deficit. At the start of the 1990s, the United States owed China about $10 billion. By 2010, that number had swelled to just over $273 billion. Other economies, in particular Taiwan, Hong Kong, Singapore, and South Korea, prospered as they helped China, India, and Thailand develop.

Pessimists see the fiercely competitive battles for trade and investment flows as evidence that the world has entered into a zero-sum game. Nothing could be further from the truth, for the simple reason that the pie is expanding at an extraordinary rate. This period brings epic opportunity to the people of the South—and no shortage of opportunities for the businesses of the North with the skill and gumption to pursue them.

. . .

This book is both a guide and a tool kit to help you make a difference in your company. It is intended to open your eyes to the dynamism that is tilting the globe from North to South. It will, I hope, enable you to go beyond rhetoric and generalities such as complaints about China's "unfair" advantages and challenge the outdated assumptions and wishful thinking that so often block leaders from seeing the immense opportunities that lie outside their line of sight. Its ultimate purpose is to show how you can share in the stupendous opportunities offered by what could be the greatest change in business history.

Make no mistake: for most business people, the tilt will present the biggest challenge of their careers. The next chapter will explain the seemingly unstoppable forces of change that drive the tilt, and help you to understand why they matter to your business. Reading on, you'll see first-hand the formidable spirit and skills of leaders in the South who are taking advantage of these trends to put their companies on the global stage.

The second part of the book gives you practical advice for succeeding in the tilt. You'll learn why old ways of thinking about strategy fall short in this environment, and why you may need to jettison your beliefs about core competencies so that you can consider making bolder moves, maybe even a big strategic bet (Chapter 4). You'll need to hone different leadership skills, including especially the "soft" ones crucial to managing what I call the social systems of the organization (Chapter 5). You'll discover why the shifts in power, resources, and behavior should be in place within your organization even before a change in structure (Chapter 6). Finally, in Chapter 7, you will pick up pointers and ideas from several companies of the North that are meeting the challenges of the tilt.

I urge you to spend the energy and time to learn about the tilt, its forces, its impact, and its speed. Form an integrated picture of the changing external landscape. You'll find a clearer path and make better decisions and be well prepared to lead.

CHAPTER TWO

WHAT YOU NEED TO KNOW FIRST

Today your company is confronting forces that are powerful and unpredictable. They range from instabilities in the global financial system to technological upheaval and abrupt changes in government policy. At the same time, the rapid growth of the South offers big opportunities.

This chapter explains these forces and shows what they mean for you. It is necessarily long because there are many factors to take into account, but it is essential reading. The successful leaders I've observed in the North and the South have a broad and penetrating view of what is happening beyond the borders of their home country. They master the global external environment. They are attuned to the shifts in the economic power of various countries, to the various trends that are shaping and reshaping markets, society, and the composition of GDP, and to changing demographics that put pressure on resources.

Such mastery is the basis of the successes you will read about later in this book and the prerequisite for determining what strategic and organizational changes you need to make. If you are too impatient, intimidated, indifferent, or arrogant to build this competence, your leadership is at risk of being obsolete. I can't say it too strongly: Whether you're a CEO or on the front line interacting directly with customers, you simply cannot plan and operate without a solid grasp of the dynamics and rules emerging in the global external environment and causing the tilt. They are changing every facet of the world you do business in. You have to step back from the constraining details of your business and industry, view the world at large, and pick out the key trends or items that could upend the world you're accustomed to and create once-in-a-lifetime opportunities.

In my view, the most important forces driving change are the global financial system; competition among countries playing by different rules; the expanding footprints of digitization and mobile communications and the wave of innovation they unleash; changing demographics; and the pressure on resources and their prices. Each alone is enough to disrupt your future, but you can't just look at them singly, as discrete phenomena, because they all influence one another. If you don't understand their interrelationships, they can sabotage your planning.

Your goal is to get to a higher altitude. It's like the view from a plane, as opposed to the one from a car. From this perspective you can see the true character of external changes. Create a network of people you can trust, including peers in other industries and organizations, to pool observations and collectively analyze the fast-changing environment. You will want people who are diverse in their thinking, backgrounds, and appetites for risk. You can create scenarios, decide which you think is most likely, and watch closely to see if you've judged them correctly.

As you become more attuned to the external environment, you'll get better at detecting not only unstoppable trends but also seemingly small hinge events—for example, the introduction of a groundbreaking product by a nontraditional competitor or new legislation—that challenge your assumptions and change the game. Your ability to see these complex shifts—either ahead of others or more accurately—will improve. You'll get better at anticipating the actions and reactions of competitors and countries. And your psychology will shift from feeling overwhelmed and anxious to enjoying the confidence and self-assurance of a leader.

A FINANCIAL SYSTEM AT RISK

Let's start with the global financial system. Nothing else keeps all the countries in the world so intricately connected or plays such an enormous role in driving the global economy. But the system is also the biggest cause of uncertainty and volatility in the real economy (the one of goods and services) because it has no central governing body and no set of enforceable rules.

There are four essential facts to keep in mind: It is huge. It has been growing with breathtaking speed. It is so interconnected, complex, and lacking in transparency that even experienced experts struggle to understand it; quite possibly nobody in the world does. And more than ever before, it is frighteningly unstable.

Start by considering how much it has grown since 2000. According to research from the McKinsey Global Institute, the total value of the world's financial stock, comprising equity market capitalization and outstanding bonds and loans, more than doubled to $196 trillion in 2007. The financial crisis knocked that back to $175 trillion in 2008, but by the end of 2010 the total had risen to $212 trillion. Cross-border capital flows have yet to recover lost ground; they grew from $5.8 trillion in 2000 to $11.2 trillion in 2007; in 2010 they amounted to just $4.4 trillion.[1]

Many players direct those flows of money. Besides banks and traditional investors, private equity firms from the United States, London, and Europe have shifted their focus south. Despite frequent restrictions against the majority stakes they're accustomed to in the North, they've been setting up special units to focus on investments in places such as China and India, providing the seed money for Southern companies to expand. Sovereign wealth adds to the firepower, especially when it teams up with private equity firms or hedge funds. Three-quarters of all such money is in the Middle East or Asia, much of it accumulated from the sale of natural resources like oil or, in the case of China, the result of its massive trade surplus, much of it with the United States. According to a report from the Sovereign Wealth Fund Institute, Bahrain, Kuwait, Oman, Qatar, Saudi Arabia, and the UAE had some $1.4 trillion assets under management in March 2010. The biggest sovereign wealth fund (SWF) of all is the Abu Dhabi Investment Authority (ADIA), which had some $650 billion in assets in the fall of 2011. Singapore, Norway, Venezuela, and China also have sizable funds. Many are managed by the world's best financial advisers, such as BlackRock, which seek investment opportunities globally.

These sources can combine, for example, through partnerships, to create even bigger flows of money to fund investments of unprecedented scale, able to help turn a small competitor into a global powerhouse practically overnight. Or they can move in unison, wreaking havoc with exchange rates, the stock market, and a nation's export-import balance. For example, when money managers begin to lose confidence in a nation, they can pull their funds out of it in a day—more rapidly than at any time in history—causing a devastating loss in liquidity and the attending panic. The flow of credit comes to a halt, precipitating a decline in the real economy, the situation in Greece and Spain as of this writing.

Mobile capital has driven growth around the world and in particular has fueled the tilt, expanding the economies of countries throughout the South. China is the showcase: Multinational companies from Hong Kong, the United States, Taiwan, Europe, and Japan began investing significantly there in the early 1990s, when China's economy was small and its trade surplus minuscule. More than half of China's exports at that point were from non-Chinese companies that took advantage of differences in labor costs and currencies—"arbitrage" is the economists' word for seeking advantage from such differences. Even as labor costs and the value of its currency, the yuan, gradually rose, China's huge markets and fast-developing manufacturing expertise continued to draw capital.

The speed and efficiency with which money moves around the world is a genuine marvel. But it has a dark side: volatility. Interest rate differences measured in fractions of a percentage point attract large inflows of foreign capital from one geography or asset class to another, in search of higher returns. In today's digitized world, those who control capital can have access to much the same information instantaneously. Computerized algorithms steer much of the trading, so traders often move in tandem, creating asset bubbles and busts or sudden swings in local currencies or the prices of commodities.

Countries attempt to protect their economies from the damaging effects of such swings by controlling the flow of speculative capital. China exercises an enormous amount of control, including all inflows and outflows of capital. In addition, its roughly $3 trillion of reserves provides a strong negotiating weapon and buffer against disruption to its domestic economy. India's government also carefully regulates foreign institutional investment (FII) and foreign direct investment (FDI), as do the nations burned by the 1997 "Asian Contagion," when Thailand had to decouple the baht from the dollar because it didn't have enough foreign-exchange reserves to support a fixed rate. The baht's collapse set off a chain reaction of devaluations and financial losses in Southeast Asia and Japan. It took two years and a $40 billion IMF currency-stabilization program for the afflicted economies to begin recovering.

But it is practically impossible to confine the flow

of capital or to isolate its effects completely. For example, when the Federal Reserve pumped $600 billion into the financial system in 2010 through quantitative easing ("QE2" in shorthand: the policy of buying up government bonds to increase the money supply), some of that money soon found its way to the higher interest rates of Hong Kong, where the Hang Seng Index surged and property values inflated. So much money poured into Brazil that its finance minister declared his country to be the victim of a "currency war." As prices inflated and industrial output began to slow, Brazil imposed a 6 percent tax on bond inflows. Thailand took a similar tack to curb the inflow of money: a 15 percent tax on interest and capital gains from government and state-owned company bonds.

In October 2012, International Monetary Fund managing director Christine Lagarde warned that easy money from the central banks of the United States and other developing countries was creating a risk of "asset price bubbles" in emerging countries.[2]

Some forms of control—for example, manipulation to keep a currency artificially low in order to boost exports—are generally considered unfair trade practices. But recognizing the new reality, in 2011 the International Monetary Fund, which has long pushed for free flows of capital, set out guidelines legitimizing controls when a country is unable to use monetary or fiscal policy to shield itself from an onslaught. "'Our policy advice clearly cannot exclude a whole swath of economic policies—still less an area where the benefits of getting it right are significant, the economic and financial risks of getting it wrong are large, and the potential global gains from internalizing multilateral considerations substantial,' said [now former] IMF managing director Dominique Strauss-Kahn."[3]

WHY MONEY IS MOVING SOUTH

Meanwhile, capital investment in hard assets continues to flow. Mostly it runs south as Northern companies shift their investment in plants, warehouses, logistics chains, and retail outlets. Over the past decade much of the money went to Brazil, Russia, India, and China—the so-called BRIC nations. More recently, reflecting the continuing roster of nations emerging into developing status, the hot new targets include Colombia, Indonesia, Vietnam, Egypt, Turkey, and South Africa (CIVETS). Barring a global calamity, new countries will continue to join the party for decades to come.

Although North to South is the general trend, the picture is not that simple. Some capital flows against the tide as Southern companies seek access to the North's huge markets and know-how. The flow from South to North is likely to increase as Southern companies search for bargain-priced companies lamed by the forces of the tilt. Capital can even flow both ways in the same industry, if two players with different strategies each see greener grass on the other side. In late 2011, for example, Gap announced that it planned to close a fifth of its stores in the United States and triple its stores in China. Even as Gap was pruning at home, its Japanese rival Uniqlo was building stores there—despite its relatively slow growth, the U.S. economy is still huge.

As companies of the South seek capital to grow, they often tap funding from multiple sources inside and outside their home countries. For example, in late 2011, India's Reliance Power Limited received government approval to borrow $2.2 billion from U.S. and Chinese banks to partially fund a power project. Also, today globally connected providers of capital form partnerships and seek mega-opportunities in the South for investments. That's why Bharti Airtel was able to buy Zain for an enterprise valuation of $10.7 billion; bankers who saw the growth potential were more than happy to fund the company's global expansion.

Cross-border investment in financial assets—foreign institutional investment (FII)—is tilting to the South along with foreign direct investment (FDI, investment by corporations in hard assets). Stock exchanges have blossomed, and investors worldwide have been drawn there for the usual reason: the tremendous opportunities for growth. The heavy influx of money in recent years has driven up price-earnings ratios to the extent that some North-based companies list their subsidiaries in the South to benefit from the difference.

These movements of capital heavily influence which geographies and which sectors of the economy are going to grow and develop and which will be starved. A flood of money is not always a blessing, though, if the hunger for growth creates excessive risk taking or overcapacity. By destroying entry barriers, excess capital can ruin the rate of return on investment for an entire industry, as happened to the airline industry in America, Europe, and India. Foreign institutional investment also affects currency valuations, balance of payments, and geopolitical relationships. China's immense sovereign-wealth investments in U.S. Treasury notes helped sustain the West's appetite for consumption and suppressed the value of China's yuan. Sovereign wealth from the Middle East rescued U.S. and British financial firms after the meltdown. Such relationships link the fates of the countries involved and change the power dynamic.

China's trade surplus has steepened the tilt by channeling money directly into companies that compete against the North. The Chinese government owns majority stakes in some of the country's largest companies.

These state-owned enterprises (SOEs) represent some 30 percent of all industrial assets in China and are run by managers in tune with the central government's goals and policies. Other countries have used their foreign earnings for the same purpose. In 1976 the government of Saudi Arabia created the Saudi Basic Industries Corporation (SABIC), taking a 70 percent stake. SABIC is now one of the world's largest manufacturers of petroleum-based products and is aggressively expanding globally. It's acquiring technology—it bought GE Plastics in 2007—and moving into growth markets, for example through joint ventures in China with Chinese company Sinopec.

There's another way in which the South has better access to investment capital: Southern companies and their owners are more patient about getting their returns than are those in the North. "Short-termism"—an excessive focus on short-term results—is the driving force for U.S. institutional investors, which hold the lion's share of all U.S. equities. Wall Street's obsession with quarterly profits favors companies that basically divest their futures, even at the expense of the long-term health of the business and domestic economy. Judgment doesn't play much of a role; proprietary econometric models ("black boxes") direct money to or away from a sector, industry, or specific company. CEO pay incentives in most companies mainly reward leaders for meeting short-term performance goals, and those who don't play to the tune of the capital-market dancing masters are often criticized and replaced. As long as the financial-services industry maintains its power over the real economies of the North, competitors from the South can build for the future while their Northern competitors are forced to forgo similar opportunities.

DANGEROUS INSTABILITY

Once you see the interconnectedness of the global financial system and its importance to worldwide economic well-being, you can begin to understand why its instability is frightening. It's a problem not just for financiers but also for Main Street corporations and individuals everywhere; and it has been compounded by the lack of political will of various government players to confront the forces that are causing uncertainty. The financial crisis that began in 2007 and reached its pinnacle in September 2008 revealed the instability and unmanageability of the system for all to see. Worse, it accelerated the tilt because it undermined Northern economies by vastly increasing government debt, raising unemployment, stifling consumption, and shrinking investment. It battered the confidence of the business community, which later became gun-shy about investing any cash it was holding. It exacerbated political turmoil in the North, drawing attention away from the

South's growing power, and in particular, the fact that the U.S. trade deficit was largely with one country: China. Indeed, I consider it an epochal transformative event, the effects of which will continue to create challenges for business and political leaders for years to come.

The crisis generated a flurry of follow-on activity in Washington, including the Dodd-Frank financial reform bill, efforts to sharpen the scrutiny of regulatory agencies, and, perhaps most important, continuing analysis and disclosures about what went wrong and what problems remain. (See the appendix "The Global Financial Crisis: Who Dealt This Mess?" at the end of this chapter for my analysis of what caused the crisis.) But realistically, a true fix is nowhere in sight. You have to prepare yourself for further problems.

The seeds of the crisis lay in the insatiable drive of Wall Street firms to maximize the shareholder value of their own firms, gaining the highest leverage permitted with novel techniques of securitization. A key player was the essentially unregulated so-called shadow banking system, which includes the $2.6 trillion U.S. money market industry. No one thought about how the unrestricted actions of individual players might combine to affect the entire system. Systemic thinking, in a nutshell, was (and still is) totally absent, so that—for example—no thought was given to the fact that some 80 percent of the risk of toxic financial instruments was flowing to one organization, AIG. It was like sludge seeping from multiple tributaries into the same narrow river, eventually clogging the flow. Compounding the problem was the philosophy of then-chairman of the Federal Reserve Alan Greenspan, who believed that markets would correct themselves. That point of view was shared by then-President George W. Bush.

The system that affects the lives of countless people around the world continues to be overseen by totally uncoordinated players. Governance of the global financial system largely lies with U.S. regulatory agencies, presidential administrations, and Congress. Its effectiveness suffers from several drawbacks. Oversight is split among multiple agencies; besides being uncoordinated, they are outsmarted by the much better-paid talent of the firms they are supposed to regulate. Moreover, there's a constant shuffle of people between the financial-services industry and the regulatory agencies. A score of executives from Goldman Sachs alone have either taken jobs at the Federal Reserve, the Treasury Department, and other agencies or been hired by Goldman from these agencies during the past three administrations. Two of the most prominent include Clinton Treasury secretary Robert Rubin and Bush Treasury secretary Hank Paulson, who led the bailout program in 2008 and appointed former Goldman vice president Neel Kashkari to oversee the $700 billion TARP fund. While it's important for the agencies to have expertise and intimate knowledge of the financial system, the revolving door between the big banks and the regulators does not make for the most objective or effective governance. Legislation is filtered through a number of congressional committees short on expertise and in thrall to special interests.

Even regulators striving to do the right thing, particularly the Federal Reserve, can be undercut by private players. They're caught up in a cat-and-mouse game with the far more powerful market players. They must take these players into account when they make their decisions, because the players try to anticipate what the regulators, especially the central bank, will do so they can plan their next moves. Their next moves may nullify the banks' efforts.

Several stakeholders outside the system itself and with no legal authority—most notably the financial ratings agencies such as Moody's, Standard & Poor's, and Fitch—have enormous influence on it. Their assessments of financial conditions affect the availability and cost of capital available to nations, industries, and companies. A ratings downgrade can cause a sharp drop in a company's stock price or increase its borrowing costs. Yet there is no accountability when these firms make the wrong judgments, as they did when they gave junk securities a top triple-A rating before the financial crisis. Further, the global financial system is dangerously opaque. Trades of enormous magnitude are made outside public view through program trading and so-called dark pools—mostly algorithm-driven computerized block trades made outside central exchanges and thus not in public view and invisible to regulators—allowing concentrations of risk to accumulate under the radar. It's one of the major reasons that markets cannot correct themselves; not all players are playing by the same rules of the game. Regulatory agencies' back-office systems and technology are no match for state-of-the-art processors that trade in nanoseconds.

Finally, control of the financial markets is concentrated in a small number of extremely powerful firms. In *Predator Nation*, his account of the financial crisis, Charles H. Ferguson writes: "By the time the bubble started, American financial services were dominated by five independent investment banks, four huge financial conglomerates, three insurers, and three ratings agencies."[4] A number were so big that the collapse of any one could endanger the entire financial system. Moreover, Ferguson adds, "many individual markets were and remain even more concentrated than the whole industry. Five institutions control over 95 percent of all derivatives trading worldwide, and two—Goldman Sachs and JPMorgan Chase—control nearly half. A group of about a dozen banks controls the LIBOR—the rate used to set nearly all short-term interest rates. . . . The top five investment banks dominate the market for initial public offerings, frequently share portions of such offerings with each other, and charge exactly the same fee."[5]

Some who are in the know tell me that the key decisions in the global financial system are made by a cozy group of fifty or fewer people from these firms. They move frequently from one company to another. Often one company poaches an entire team from another. Over time they have built informal social networks, not just among themselves but also with regulators, most of whom have been employees of these companies or will go to these companies once their short tenure in government is over.

THINKING IT THROUGH FOR YOURSELF

Going forward, your understanding of how the global financial system works will help you navigate through the complexities and uncertainties using your own good judgment. You will be able to follow the trends in the availability of capital and the overall direction of its flow as well as watch for pockets of excess that might cause a break in the system. You may think, *Best to leave that to the experts,* but you'd be wrong. You are as well equipped as the experts to do this for three basic reasons.

First, the most respected experts, even those whose research and views are promulgated in the business press, are specialists. They look at the financial system through the lens of the narrow discipline in which they have been trained. Their insights are often tremendous and deep, but their interpretations are from the viewpoint of their area of expertise rather than the total system. Second, almost all of these specialists hold to a specific ideology. One is that markets will correct themselves, so the government shouldn't intervene. The opposing ideology is that only regulation can prevent and correct problems. The specialists in both camps make assumptions based on their beliefs that get embedded in their mathematical models. The assumptions become opaque, and the models focus on narrow aspects of the financial system. Third, much of the information that rolls out from government and private sources is qualitative and ambiguous; the appearance of precision is often false. U.S. unemployment statistics, for example, are notoriously fickle. Almost all information from China is unreliable.

You are better off using the insight and information the experts provide to form your own view of the total system, seeing patterns at the highest level and crystallizing what really matters. Keep in mind that this is not your old environment, where you work with established, familiar norms and have developed an instinct for ferreting out the information that counts. You will need to sift through a ton of factors to select the crucial few. Go through permutations and combinations and connect them to get insight. Many people brainstorm with others to test their hypotheses; the key is to make judgments about whom can be trusted. With practice, you will hone your skills and derive your own meaning.

For example, suppose that you make automobiles in Brazil. What does it mean to you when large amounts of money flow into the country? The cars will become more expensive compared with imports, since the currency is being revalued. This could go on for a long time, ravaging your industry. What might you do to save your hide? Cutting costs won't be enough, but maybe the government could help—not with bailouts or the like but with a policy change that would impose duties on the imports. Why would the government want to do this? You need to assemble a delegation of peers in the industry who can show what the consequences will be for the country if nothing is done.

How about an opportunity instead? You're the CEO of an Indian company with half of its revenue in dollars and no debt, facing the same forces. If you are tracking the global financial system, you might see that you have a brilliant strategic option to go forward. With interest rates at or near all-time lows, you could raise funds through long-term borrowing in U.S. dollars and use the money to make a strategic acquisition that's a once-in-a-lifetime chance to take your company to a new level.

THE STATE INTERVENES

Political scientist Ian Bremmer relates a telling story at the beginning of his book *The End of the Free Market*.[6] The scene is a meeting in New York in 2009 between a group of economists and scholars and China's vice foreign minister, He Yafei. Writes Bremmer: "The smiling vice minister began the meeting with a question: 'Now that the free market has failed,' he asked, 'what do you think is the proper role for the state in the economy?'"

As Mark Twain said about rumors of his death, the pronouncement is premature. Most countries continue to permit market forces to drive their economies. And those forces are always regulated and guided to some degree—the pure, utterly free markets imagined by economic romantics are nowhere to be found in reality. Even America, the free-market champion of the world, has some forms of protectionism, such as agricultural subsidies.

But outright protectionism is now commonplace and is going far beyond the economists' classic examples of import tariffs and quotas to include such things as limits on equity stakes, requirements for local content, certification approvals that favor local businesses, restrictions on exports, currency manipulation, and, perhaps most insidious, massive government support for chosen businesses and industries. By comparison, previous efforts have been small potatoes. Mechanisms such as the World Trade Organization smoothed the occasionally ruffled feathers over claims of unfair subsidies and the like, and trade agreements eased the free flow of goods and services.

The extent of these controls reflects the political architecture of a nation, which ranges from the minimalist role of the U.S. government to the ironclad authoritarianism of Cuba and North Korea, modeled on Soviet-era communism. Generally speaking, a democratic architecture means less control, but not always. Singapore, for example, is a democracy, but its voters support a government that has substantial powers to shape and direct business activity.

As countries vie for advantage, businesses get caught in the crossfire. For example, in 2011 the Brazilian government used its stake in a mining company, Vale, to force a change in leadership and further its national economic development goals. Despite a successful ten-year tenure and support from investors, Vale CEO Roger Agnelli was pushed out of office because he was focusing on China rather than investing locally in job-creating industries such as steel, shipbuilding, and fertilizer. Nationalism won out over what appeared to be sound business practice.

Bremmer's label for highly hands-on direction of an economy is "state capitalism." If governments practicing state capitalism can execute, they can have one notable advantage in the global marketplace: decisiveness. Some countries can execute better than others. Democracies, with their need to balance conflicting views and demands, will move slowly in the face of domestic divisions. Indeed, they can become so indecisive as to be almost paralyzed, as in the cases of Japan and Italy, owing to their political architecture. Lately the United States has fallen into a similar gridlock because of its highly polarized politics. Democracies, it seems, act swiftly and decisively only when they face real or perceived national emergencies that draw their fractious constituents together.

THE CHALLENGE OF CHINESE CAPITALISM

No country practices state capitalism more skillfully and aggressively than China. Because it is destined to overtake the United States in GDP in the not-so-distant future, you should understand in some detail how the country operates. China's approach marks the first time in modern history that a nation has the economic clout of a major trading partner yet relies on the competitive tactics of an upstart. Its version of state capitalism is particularly effective because it combines several elements: well-informed and pragmatic planning by world-class experts, including consultants from the North; a political architecture that coordinates governmental bodies and holds them accountable; an execution machine with rewards and punishments from central levels to the local level; and a hybrid form of business enterprise that blends business and government.

China defends its intense government involvement in building businesses by pleading necessity. Its goals are staggeringly ambitious: continuing the transformation of a nation with a current population of almost 1.4 billion people from poverty to prosperity, while at the same time expanding personal freedom in a controlled, incremental fashion. Its leaders are deeply—and not unrealistically—afraid of social unrest that could derail its phased transition into the modern economic world, and so they do all they can to keep jobs growing. These days, for instance, the increasing income gap between the rural and urban populations is driving a program to create new, smaller urban centers anchored around manufacturing.

But China's actions also reflect broader global intentions: to make the yuan a reserve currency, build extraordinary financial reserves, secure natural resources from around the world—and be a world leader. Its immediate focus is on economic power. For example, through the building of roads, ports, and pipelines, it has shown its intent to funnel trade flows with the South into the Chinese heartland. With economic power comes political power.

Singapore was a valuable model for China. From Lee Kuan Yew, Singapore's first premier, the Chinese learned the strategy of building an export-based economy: Bring manufacturing in with wage and currency arbitrage, then move up the value chain; be sure to put competent people in charge, with pay incentives linked to economic performance. But China far surpassed the master in guiding capitalism to the state's advantage and also put into practice one additional piece of advice: Build foreign reserves that will shield you from the unpredictability and wild swings of democratic capitalist societies.

A DIFFERENT KIND
OF CENTRAL PLANNING

China makes its economic priorities explicit and targets specific industries to develop in its five-year plan, a comprehensive document that lays out everything the state hopes to achieve in the coming period in great detail. It is now executing its twelfth five-year plan. One of the stated goals is to develop seven "strategic emerging industries": alternative energy, biotechnology, new-generation information technology, high-end equipment manufacturing, advanced materials, alternative-fuel cars, and energy-saving and environmental protection. (It has already become the world's largest maker of wind turbines and solar panels.) "Five-year plan" conjures up memories of the old Soviet Union's recurring central planning failures, but China's plans have nothing in common with those fantasies. Instead they are pragmatic undertakings built on factual information, compiled and executed by highly educated experts working with rigorous analytics and methodologies—and held accountable for the outcome of their work.

As Kenneth G. Lieberthal of the Brookings Institution explains in his 2010 book *Managing the China Challenge*, a top-down appointment system ensures that every political and party leader is sensitive to the goals and concerns of the leaders directly above him or her. Lower-level leaders control the bureaucratic agencies in their own jurisdictions, the courts, and local bank branches. They can decide the outcomes of legal decisions of real concern to them and dictate which local bank branches will provide credit to which projects. They can promote the growth of favored enterprises in their local jurisdictions through such means as granting business licenses (and changing them) and making available land and below-market-rate credit.[7] This arrangement gives a Chinese mayor considerable power over multinational companies that compete against indigenous companies.

Local control is tightly linked to China's central plan. Chinese government officials retain or do not retain their jobs based on how well they contribute to the goals of the leaders above them. They are assessed in writing every year, and here's what's especially revealing: According to Lieberthal, about 60 percent of the metrics that have been used to measure performance have directly or indirectly reflected GDP growth over the previous year. The system isn't perfect, but it has been effective.

The line between business and government disappears with China's state-owned enterprises (SOEs). Unconstrained by the need to turn profits, they are primarily vehicles for advancing national self-interest, for example, by procuring raw materials abroad. Chinese SOEs spent more than $100 billion buying mining and energy companies over the past five years[8] and more than $5 billion to secure copper from places like Afghanistan and Zambia. In 2011 a consortium of five state-owned companies bought a 15 percent stake in the world's largest producer of niobium, a hard-to-come-by metal used to strengthen steel for such things as jet engine components and superconductor materials. In 2012, China National Offshore

Oil Corporation (CNOOC) made a $15.1 billion offer to acquire Nexen, one of Canada's largest energy producers, a company with capabilities at the frontier of energy extraction, including drilling for natural gas in shale rock and deep-sea drilling in the Gulf of Mexico.

DO WE HAVE A WINNER?

Is China's version of state capitalism a sustainable new model? Probably not.

Some of China's huge trade surplus is due to labor arbitrage and low currency valuation, neither of which is sustainable. Already wages are on the rise in the industrial centers, and lower-cost players such as Vietnam and Bangladesh are capturing business that previously would have gone to China. This trend will inevitably continue. In some cases, production is trickling back to Northern nations. The basis of competition will increasingly shift to traditional levers, such as technological advantage and managerial prowess. While some private Chinese companies—Haier and Huawei, for example—have built muscle as global players, SOEs have yet to prove they have an edge over North-based companies in decision making, execution, resource allocation, and innovation.

The core problem is the classic flaw of any economy where government dictates investment policies: politics tends not to respect the efficient deployment of capital. Showering unearned money on enterprises is usually wasteful (a mistake the North makes too when government picks a favored "industry of the future" to subsidize). China's system for allocating capital to SOEs has produced some winners, to be sure, but it's also created spectacular losers. For example, as Bill Powell wrote in *Fortune* magazine: "China's solar energy industry has become nothing less than a capital destruction machine, with some of its most prominent companies now desperately flailing for lifelines." The same is true of most Northern solar companies, driven to the wall by China's low-priced output. Powell cites research by the Sanford Bernstein securities firm to suggest that "solar is turning into the DRAM industry: a business which for decades was a capital intensive, low profit tong war, waged between Japanese competitors and, later, Korean companies, led by Samsung—which eventually emerged as the clear industry leader."[9]

Of course, this could be another instance of the clash between a relatively quick payoff and the long-term rewards of patient capital. For example, Japan has now joined Germany in rejecting nuclear power, which will inevitably increase the demand for solar. In an energy market with as many uncertainties as this one, it could be a gamble that pays off eventually. But *gamble* would seem to be the key word.

China's internal stresses—for example, growing income inequality and pressures for more democracy—could throw sand in the elaborate gears and compromise its ability to execute the twelfth five-year plan. "China 2030," a World Bank report prepared in cooperation with China's Ministry of Finance and Development Research Center of the State Council, issued in June 2012, stressed that structural reforms to create a market-based economy are critical to the country's success. Among them are rebalancing growth toward domestic consumption and away from investment and exports, and—most notably—cutting back China's state-owned enterprises and giving more support to private enterprise. However, until its domestic economy can absorb the prodigious output of its factories, China's policies are unlikely to change much. Quelling social unrest will likely require expanding inter-party democracy, a delicate process in a system that permits little political input from its citizens. President Hu has been vocal about opening the nation to diverse voices, but so far experimentation has been strictly at the local level.

How China's leaders deal with these issues could alter the speed and direction of the tilt from North to South. After some three decades of GDP growth averaging about 10 percent annually, the pace of China's growth is generally expected to average 8 percent or less over the next several years.

As to the putative failure of the free market, the United States has a track record more than two centuries long, and has been a model for most of the world's successful economies. It operates on the premise that freedom of choice and secure property rights are what enable individuals to create economic growth, and business leaders to exercise initiative and make their companies flourish through innovation, productivity gains, close attention to their markets, and new business models. New initiatives and new technologies can flourish because of highly sophisticated institutions that have the expertise and willingness to fund risky projects—and de-fund those that can't earn their way.

While technologies can be bought or copied, their deep and institutionalized wellsprings are difficult if not impossible to duplicate. Silicon Valley, for instance, is an institution in itself, an intellectual community of unsurpassed talent and collaboration. In addition, these advantages are supported by the world's most advanced educational institutions, a relatively mobile workforce, and the effective melding of diverse people from other nations. Just as important, the same institutions that fund risky projects are quick to *de*-fund those that don't earn adequate returns on capital. Government-supported companies, by contrast, most often don't have this check on their ambitions. They don't have the same imperative to develop the muscles of productivity, innovation, and competitiveness. And they aren't impelled to develop competent leadership.

Finally, keep in mind a quote generally attributed to Winston Churchill: "Attitude is a little thing that can make a big difference." Americans have always understood that they live in a place where a nobody can still become a somebody.

America's current challenge is its lack of a coherent plan for solving the trade and federal deficits and promoting its economic power through long-term investments in such essentials as infrastructure, education, and basic research. The division of powers inherent in the American political system has made democracy viable over the long haul. But bitter partisan battles have put it at a big disadvantage in comparison with the focus and effectiveness of China's guided capitalism. Once the United States overcomes its political gridlock and arrives at consensus on a national economic agenda, its businesses will be better supported and trade imbalances will improve. And as it moves toward energy independence by developing its shale gas and "tight oil," it will not only reap huge revenues and create vast numbers of jobs; it will also have more strategic leverage in the world.

Innovation, productivity improvement, new business creation, and individual and state initiatives are alive and well, as is the sine qua non of a democratic society, leadership from below. Many states stimulate their economies with focused programs that invite foreign direct investment that creates jobs. People in these states have elected politicians who moderate local laws and state expenditures to create an environment more conducive to building a business, thereby improving the employment picture, tax base, and overall frame of mind about the future. It will take just a small core of leaders from both the executive office and the legislature who bridge the gap at the level of national policy to change the trajectory. A workable consensus in the areas of taxes, infrastructure, innovation, education, immigration, and regulation—like the one reached during the financial crisis with passage of the Troubled Asset Relief Program (TARP)—will create the opportunity for America to pick up the pace and regain its economic and technological leadership in the eyes of the world.

Business, of course, has its own major role to play, by itself and in conjunction with government and academia. Useful advice comes from Harvard Business School's Competitiveness Project, which has put together a multipoint plan for businesses to pursue, ranging from continued devotion to productivity to improving skills, upgrading supporting industries, and reining in self-interested behaviors that in the aggregate detract from economic performance.[10]

The tug-of-war will continue, especially in times of slow growth. Advantages will come and go. But the world is still growing. For all of the trouble and angst it causes Northern nations and businesses, China's success is also creating huge opportunities and driving the other economies of the South closer to one another. For you as a business leader, long-term success in the tilt means staying alert to the tactics countries use to bolster their own economies while building a business strong enough to win customers now and in the future.

DIGITIZATION: IT WILL REVOLUTIONIZE YOUR BUSINESS

The changes flowing from digitization are so continual and fast that trying to grasp their overall impact is like trying to gauge weather patterns while standing in a hailstorm. Many of the details are familiar: digital technology lowers cost and shortens cycle time; it allows companies to reach high volumes and generate cash quickly without a lot of capital; it pinpoints market segments and individual customers; it disrupts traditional marketing and distribution channels and radically changes relationships between businesses and consumers . . . and the list goes on. But here's the big picture: digitization is making opportunity more ubiquitous, allowing new forms of value creation, and changing the composition of the global economy. It will increasingly alter value chains, eliminating intermediary links and upending old notions about scale economies.

Many current assumptions are already under assault. Take, for example, commoditization, the fear that haunts almost every business. Digital technology has widened and accelerated the threat. Yet just now emerging is a new generation of digital technologies that portend the exact opposite: the de-commoditization of product lines. Versatile and flexible computer-driven machinery can produce ever smaller batches of product—all the way down to batches of one—at costs not much greater than those of large-scale production. For example, using so-called 3-D printing, or "additive" manufacturing technology, machines shape material into whatever configurations the computer code tells them to. Instead of retooling equipment for each change, manufacturers need only to reset computer codes to produce a different item. The impact promises to be profound. Businesses will increasingly be able to build products where the customers are, instead of in big plants hundreds or thousands of miles away. As it develops, this trend is likely to speed the innovation cycle, redefine supply chain and distribution logistics, drive costs down further, and make wider varieties of goods available to more people. And it may erode some of the South's advantages. Almost needless to say, it will force businesses to rethink their operations and planning.

Another huge result of digitization is the ability to create an entire new global industry from scratch in just a few years. Companies including Google, Vonage, Skype, and Apple are moving into the flow of telecommunications and creating cross-industry disruption. They have already begun to capture voice and data portions of the growing industry revenue earned by telecom carriers, and there's reason to think that their portion will grow. In addition to their cost advantage, they aren't bound by any legacy mind-set—and unlike their competitors, they are unregulated.

Internet-based marketing is still rewriting established rules of selling. Amazon, which may be the most sophisticated Internet company in the world, has not only an impregnable cost structure and delivery method, but an unsurpassed ability to understand and target its customers with algorithms that track their buying habits. After shaking up the bricks-and-mortar bookstore business model, it is doing the same in consumer goods ranging from apparel to appliances, challenging retailers such as Best Buy and even Walmart; suddenly the onetime maverick in retailing is a traditional player under assault.

Add mobile technology to the picture. Consumers get

information about where to buy, learning, for example, that as they walk toward Main Street there's a shoe store just a block away. They can call up a variety of reviews, including those by fellow consumers, compare prices, and then go online to buy what they've seen—cheaper and with free delivery. These engagements create revenue-generating opportunities for some, destroy them for others, and squeeze a lot of capital investment out of the value and supply chains.

Social networking is another game-changer, though the game is still one of guessing. We know that it can spread new ideas and influence behaviors on a massive scale, in moments. It can do everything from creating instant new markets for consumer products to unseating governments (think Arab Spring). Facebook's disappointing IPO in 2012 made clear that many questions remain about how powerful a marketing tool social networking can become. But its potential seems vast; businesses are only beginning to explore ways of using it to pinpoint and satisfy consumer desires—and, with mobile phone apps, in real time.

The ability to compile and manipulate increasingly large data sets—so-called big data—promises to dramatically reshape business activity. The McKinsey Global Institute calls it the next frontier for innovation, competition, and productivity, adding: "The use of big data will underpin new waves of productivity growth and consumer surplus." For example, says McKinsey, "We estimate that a retailer using big data to the full has the potential to increase its operating margin by more than 60 percent."[11]

The explosion of big data comes from the increasing volume and detail of information captured from multimedia, social media, businesses' own operations, and the so-called Internet of Things—information from sensors embedded in physical objects ranging from pacemakers to roadways, to billboards in Japan that scan passersby to assess how they fit consumer profiles and instantly change displayed messages based on those assessments. McKinsey notes that capitalizing on this torrent of information will command the attention of not just data-oriented managers but leaders at all levels: "Organizations need not only to put the right talent and technology in place but also structure workflows and incentives to optimize the use of big data."[12]

The most dramatic change of all may be the power of digital technology to create structural changes in the composition of national economies. For example, mobile communications networks are leapfrogging the time-consuming process of extending landlines to the far reaches of places such as India and Africa, disbursing information and even medical care and increasing people's appetites for a better life.

But do those changes also portend job losses on a huge scale? Some digital-based industries can grow revenues exponentially in a very short time without creating many jobs. In their book *Race Against the Machine,* Erik Brynjolfsson and Andrew McAfee argue that "computers (hardware, software, and networks) are only going to get more powerful and capable in the future, and have an ever-bigger impact on jobs, skills, and the economy."[13] The worry arises from the growing capability of computers to replace human input in realms once considered beyond the machines' capabilities. Take pattern recognition, essentially a machine version of the human ability to learn in real time and adapt to changing conditions. Pattern recognition is the basis of the algorithms that Amazon and a host of unknown companies use to worm their way into the lives of consumers, by aggregating information gleaned from Web activities into precisely targeted sales pitches. It's noteworthy that Google, not Toyota or General Motors, modified a fleet of cars to drive thousands of miles on public roads without any human involvement. Another new humanlike computer power is complex communication—the ability to converse with human beings even in situations that are complicated, emotional, or ambiguous. Early in 2012 Citigroup announced that it was looking into uses for IBM's Watson, the supercomputer that caught the public eye when it beat two of the best contestants of the game show *Jeopardy!* IBM has partnered with the health insurance plan provider WellPoint to put Watson to work helping medical professionals diagnose treatment options for complicated health issues. And Citi, citing Watson's ability to analyze human language and process vast amounts of information, was expecting to give it a job in customer service.

From the early days of the industrial revolution onward, of course, critics of "automation" have constantly worried about the loss of jobs. Maybe this time they're right. But consider the finding from a recent Booz Allen study called "Maximizing the Impact of Digitization." Among other things, the authors measured that impact in 150 countries and came up with some striking information. "An increase in digitization of 10 percentage points triggered a 0.50 to 0.62 percent gain in per capita income," they found. "The more advanced the country, the greater the impact of digitization appears to be, which establishes a virtuous feedback cycle; a country reinforces and accelerates its own progress as it moves along the line." What about job losses? In fact, they found that digitization creates jobs: "A 10 percent increase in digitization reduces a nation's unemployment rate by 0.84 percent. From 2009 to 2010, digitization added an estimated 19 million jobs to the global economy, up from the estimated 18 million jobs added from 2007 to 2008."[14]

The one certainty today is that digitization will play an ever-expanding role in shaping economic activity. The old agenda items associated with digitization—product and process productivity and quality, portfolio adjustments to reduce capital—will be superseded. Almost all companies will need to center their strategies on innovation and the implication of digitization. It will change every ecosystem and supply chain.

INNOVATION UNLEASHED

Another characteristic of the new world economy will be invention of a type and scale never before seen. Major innovation in the latter part of the twentieth century was, for the most part, institutionalized: highly concentrated in large companies such as Intel, Motorola, Siemens, and Bell Labs and in universities such as MIT, Stanford, and Harvard, and created by a relatively small number of people, most of them experts in one discipline or another. More recently, American tech entrepreneurs have been changing the world. Prominent among them: Steve Jobs, Marc Andreessen (inventor of the browser and now Silicon Valley's most influential venture capitalist), Jeff Bezos (Amazon), and Mark Zuckerberg (Facebook).

Now a whole new population of innovators is in sight. Vast swarms of people, especially knowledge workers—

though also including some who may not even have gone to college—are innovating around the world. Their ability to do so singly and collectively comes largely from the increasing real-time openness and democratization of knowledge and availability of startup funds in a digitized world. The latest help comes from cellular communication. The world's two and a half billion mobile phone users— a number that grows daily, along with the proportion of smartphones in the mix—are able to share information they could never before access. Much of this innovation is at the local level for the local market, and some will find its way from one country to another. Online contests and crowdfunding help small-scale entrepreneurs get the money they need to develop their ideas.

The new population of innovators will also include many who work in large corporations, according to Scott D. Anthony, managing director of Innosight Asia-Pacific and author of *The Little Black Book of Innovation*.[15] "The revolution spurred by venture capitalists decades ago has created the conditions in which scale enables big companies to stop shackling innovation and start unleashing it," he writes in *Harvard Business Review*.[16] Taking a page from start-up strategy, he says, they "are embracing open innovation and less hierarchical management and are integrating entrepreneurial behaviors with their existing capabilities. . . . It's early days still, but the evidence is compelling that we are entering a new era of innovation, in which entrepreneurial individuals, or 'catalysts,' within big companies are using those companies' resources, scale, and growing agility to develop solutions to global challenges in ways that few others can."

BILLIONS OF NEW CONSUMERS

As the tilt expands the world's human needs and capabilities, businesses surveying the boundless opportunities have their eyes particularly on the exploding middle class, with its millions of new consumers. But you need to be nuanced in how you think about the middle class—it's really many different segments, and they change quickly. You will have to identify these segments and prepare for more frequent strategy changes if you hope to succeed in this diverse and constantly evolving marketplace.

Even defining "middle class" is a tricky undertaking. One respected set of estimates comes from the Brookings Institution, in a 2011 report by Homi Kharas and Geoffrey Gertz.[17] They define the global middle as households with daily expenditures between ten dollars and one hundred dollars per person in purchasing-power parity terms. But the ten-dollar threshold implies that some countries have no middle classes at all. As the *Economic Times* of India noted, "Everyone spending that much is in the top 5 percent here." Nancy Birdsall, an economist who founded the Center for Global Development in Washington, D.C., suggests a four-dollar lower limit to include what she calls a "catalyzing class" of people who are not poor but not quite middle class, with implicit opportunities for upward mobility.[18]

Using the ten-dollar figure, and drawing from available data for 145 countries accounting for 98 percent of the world's population, Kharas and Gertz reach a strikingly optimistic conclusion: "Our scenario shows that over the coming twenty years the world evolves from being mostly poor to mostly middle class. 2022 marks the first year more people in the world are middle class than poor. By 2030, 5 billion people—nearly two thirds of the global population—could be middle class."

The distribution of spending by that middle class will be significantly different from today's. Asians will spend the most. The authors note that "by 2015, for the first time in a hundred years, the number of Asian middle class consumers will equal the number in Europe and North America. By 2021, on present trends, there could be more than 2 billion Asians in middle class households. In China alone, there could be over 670 million middle class consumers, compared with only perhaps 150 million today."[19] Yet as the chart shows, raw numbers alone don't paint the complete picture: China has more people than India, but India's middle class is younger than China's and will account for a considerably larger share of global consumption by 2048. Kharas and Gertz estimate that by 2030 India will account for approximately 23 percent of global middle-class consumption, China 18 percent, the United States 7 percent, and Germany and France 2 percent each.

Consumer-goods companies from the North, such as Coca-Cola, Colgate, and Unilever, have long had a global presence, but now shoppers on every continent stream into retailers such as Wal-Mart, Uniqlo, and the Gap. Audis sell briskly in China and India, and KFC is a mainstay restaurant in places as far-flung as China and Nigeria. Local businesses in the South, both small and large, have also benefited. Indian consumer-goods company Marico has expanded its reach to several countries in Asia and the Middle East, giving its top line a 44 percent boost in five years. As these companies expand, so does the number of people on their payroll, and the middle class grows.

The tremendous demand for resources has accelerated the progress of countries that possess them. Among these are the chronically underdeveloped countries of Africa. In many, the inflow of money has combined with some degree of political reform to allow the emergence of a sizable middle class for the first time ever. Another beneficiary is

Indonesia. Japanese bank Nomura estimates the middle class of Indonesia—a large exporter of oil and coal—at fifty million, larger than India's.[20]

The great demographic shift makes a compelling case for any growth-seeking company to focus on the South. But don't paint an entire hemisphere with the same brush. India, for example, is not one economy but many, with its states of Gujarat, Maharashtra, and Karnataka far more economically advanced and likely to grow much more than Orissa or Uttar Pradesh. Bharti Airtel has defined thirty-eight distinct geographic markets in India and 106 distinct microgeographical markets in Africa called Zones. China too has big internal disparities between its relatively well-off industrial centers and its vast countryside.

There are two other important things to note about the global middle class.

First, it will increasingly be urban. Across the South, as they did earlier in the North, people have been moving to cities in large numbers, generally to escape the desperate poverty and depleted farmlands of rural villages. According to WHO, 53 percent of the world's people now live in cities. By 2050, that figure should rise to 75 percent.

From Mumbai to Shanghai to São Paulo the residents of those cities have been finding jobs linked with exports to Europe, Japan, and especially the United States, and are rising from satisfying basic needs to buying a wide range

of products and branded goods. Expanding local economies draw more people to the cities and enlarge the middle class. Those lucky enough to have a formal education
have begun to take positions as engineers, programmers,
analysts, marketers, and managers in both domestic and
foreign-owned companies.

Their spending creates all sorts of new businesses,
many with expanding opportunities of their own. And it
doesn't take a degree to become a successful entrepreneur.
A *Wall Street Journal* story datelined Lima, Peru, captured
this chain of opportunity concisely:

> Aquilino Flores was a ragged looking 13-year-old
> when he started his career hawking T-shirts in the
> barrios of this capital city. Today his company, Topi-
> top, is Peru's largest apparel maker, with a chain of
> stores extending nationwide.
>
> Over the past decade, as Peru transformed into
> one of the world's fastest growing economies, up-
> wardly mobile consumers began snapping up Topitop
> polo shirts and cargo pants made of high-quality fab-
> rics and marketed under exotic sounding labels.
>
> With stores strategically located in long-ignored
> barrios and provincial towns, Topitop's sales have ex-
> panded six-fold since 2001, earning it the nickname
> "the Andean Zara."

Shopping at a Topitop mall store in Lima recently, David Caceres, who runs a tiny car repair business here, bought a dressy pullover from the company's "New York" label and a star-emblazoned T-shirt from its edgier "Hawk" line. "I'll still have money left for movie tickets," he says.[21]

Second, the middle class will be relatively youthful. The average age in some of the largest countries of the South is considerably younger than in the North. Half the population of India is below the age of twenty-seven. Sub-Saharan Africa is younger still. China's population is relatively mature, creating tension between its need to consume and its need to save. These differences combine with cultural ones to create many marketing segments and subsegments, the composition of which can change very fast. (Visit populationpyramids.net for instant graphic depictions of these age differences.)

Note that the future of these young people depends on rising prosperity. They need jobs, and they need to be educated and trained for them. A country's GDP has to grow fast enough to absorb those coming of working age, and the education system has to keep pace. High unemployment among young people is a major source of social unrest. Consider the 20-plus percent unemployment rates across the Middle East and North Africa around the time of the Arab Spring.[22] Shirish Sankhe of McKinsey's Mumbai office explains that "India's gross domestic product needs to grow by more than 10 percent a year just to keep pace with the growth of the workforce, which is expected to increase by about one-third over the next 20 years."[23] Sankhe goes on to say, "Close to 270 million people will be entering the workforce. Yet the real job creation will be closer to 120 million to 150 million. That means the rest of the people will have to stay in agriculture."

A weak education system can put a crimp in a company's expansion plans or at least make it more costly to operate. In many high-growth countries, the supply of people trained as managers, marketers, engineers, and financial analysts has not kept up, creating a fight for talent and driving up wages. Salaries of senior managers and engineers in Brazil often match or exceed those in the United States. Some companies try to fill the void by providing training, but scarcity also affects retention. Engineers in India are known to jump ship frequently in search of a salary increase. Salary increases of 15 percent a year are normal for some jobs in India.

SPEEDILY SHIFTING SEGMENTS

For a company doing business around the world, the growth of a youthful middle class adds up to a marketplace of mind-bending diversity, with segments that constantly change and mutate. To take one example, people earning three thousand dollars a year now in China could be making six thousand in three or four years and traveling to Canada and the United States. Cross-border mobility in many regions will add to the complexity of segmentation. Companies will have to identify the needs of all these segments and work backward, rather than hoping to modify existing products. They will have to master fast changes in communications and channels to customers; they will have to pinpoint subsegments including, for example, ethnic and religious groups within a given segment, with many distinct values and tastes of their own. Mastery of the local demography and its evolution will be central to winning.

While most eyes are on the middle class, however, it is not the only large-scale game on the planet. The bifurcation of income distribution between the very wealthy and all the rest will only increase. This is an unstoppable trend: In absolute terms, the profits going to those in the upper reaches of giant organizations can only increase. They will become an ever-larger market for makers of luxury items, from clothing and homes to cars, yachts, and airplanes.

At the other end of the spectrum, companies are designing products at low price points in emerging markets. So-called frugal innovation is likely to effectively expand the middle class by increasing its purchasing power. It will also open new markets among the poor. Hindustan Unilever and Procter & Gamble, for example, have designed low-cost detergent products tailored to the needs and constraints of India's impoverished rural sections. Tata Chemical's Swach water purifier is aimed at the same market; it filters water through rice husk ash and can provide a family of five with safe water for thirty rupees (less than a dollar) a month.

JOCKEYING FOR RESOURCES

The burgeoning population of new consumers strains the world's resources, including food, water, fuel, and minerals. Human imagination and capital usually remedy imbalances between demand and supply, but they cannot always keep up in the great new spurt of prosperity. The magnitude and speed of the increases in demand, coupled with the time lag in increasing production or finding substitutes, make for a new insecurity in what used to be dependable supplies. Governments that limit exports to satisfy their own economic plans exacerbate the problem, as do increasingly large and powerful suppliers with greater control over prices. The resulting imbalances have the potential to slow seemingly unstoppable economic expansion in some places, and also to create tensions among trading partners. At the least, they sabotage strategic plans, both short- and long-term. Here again, business leaders must hone their thinking, particularly in analyzing government involvement or control that disrupts the natural market forces.

China has been the biggest disrupter as both a buyer and supplier of resources. The country's unmet needs and long planning horizon ensure that its appetite, albeit somewhat curbed by a recent slowdown in economic growth, will continue. It gets oil not just through signing contracts with suppliers: it buys the source. It needs food, so it tries to secure agricultural land outside China and fertilizer to grow it. It sends armies of Chinese workers to build railroads and ports in Africa in exchange for future supplies of such things as cobalt. Its deep pockets and long-term focus make it a Goliath against even the largest corporations that vie for resources independently.

When China exercises its power as a supplier, it can rock entire industries. Despite being a member of the WTO, which explicitly forbids export quotas, in 2010 it tightened restrictions on the export of rare earth minerals, where it had a 95 percent share of global supply, causing a worldwide scramble for the many non-Chinese companies that depend on them. Efforts by individual companies to stretch supplies and find substitutes eased but didn't eliminate concerns about China's control. In March 2012, even as prices for rare earth minerals softened along with global economic growth, the United States, Europe, and Japan filed a case with the WTO for what they claimed were unfair quotas and tariffs. At this time that case is pending. What no one could dispute was that a single entity—the Chinese government—held the cards. Even as the trade barriers eased and mining companies raced to fire up production of known deposits in other countries, businesses reckoned with the potential for more of the same.

Increasingly large and powerful private-sector suppliers exacerbate the problems. Throughout the 2000s, mining companies Vale, Rio Tinto, and BHP Billiton absorbed competitors as they raced to expand their capacities and scale. With fewer players came greater pricing power. In 2008, with demand ahead of supply, the giants of iron-ore mining began to shift toward shorter-term contracts, first quarterly, then monthly; the uncertainty played havoc with buyers' plans. In March 2010, European carmakers felt the pinch when iron-ore producers flexed their new-found muscles raising prices by more than 80 percent. Industry groups sought help from the European Commission in Brussels, claiming that the three biggest producers (Vale, Rio Tinto, and BHP Billiton accounted for 70 percent of the ore that is transported) had "the significant pricing power of an oligopoly."[24] The European Automobile Manufacturers' Association said, "Such excessive and unpredictable pricing policy would affect the competitiveness of manufacturing in Europe, including the automotive industry."[25]

To complicate things further for businesses heavily dependent on volatile resources, price hikes in times of shortage are not necessarily industry-wide; the playing field tilts depending on negotiations and relative power. And because efforts to secure them create a huge transfer of wealth to resource-rich countries and speeds their economic development, which in turn increases demand—the swings are wide with far-reaching impacts in both directions.

Another risk to key inputs comes from efforts to keep costs down: tight inventories in supply chains can create monumental disruptions if something happens to a critical component. "People aren't willing to pay to have empty capacity there just in case, because there's a cost to it," says John Hoffecker, managing director at consulting firm Alix Partners LLC.[26] That point hit home with the automotive industry in the spring of 2012 when a major supplier of a chemical crucial in automotive fuel and braking systems had a problem. Early in 2012 its plant in Marl, Germany, blew up, wiping out much of the world's production of the chemical. Knowing how tight inventories were at every link in the supply chain, executives worried that shortages would cause them to stop their production lines—an utter disaster in an industry with such tight margins. At a hastily convened meeting in Detroit, automakers and suppliers gathered to explore their options. They headed off a crisis by expediting their parts-validation process so that they could more quickly replace the resin with alternatives. But the episode provides a useful warning to all businesses heavily dependent on a single source of a critical input.

In India, a unique congeries of factors has left the country badly short of coal supplies. Coal generates more than half of the country's electricity, and is used for much of its aluminum production. About 12 percent of that coal is imported, of which 70 percent comes from Indonesia.[27] To maximize the economic benefits of its reserves, Indonesia set new rules in 2009: metal producers have to refine the ore in Indonesia before it can be exported, and international mining companies have to sell 51 percent of their mines to local companies after ten years of production.[28] In 2012, it imposed a 25 percent export tax on coal.[29]

The Indian government tries to help by negotiating for coal, but it suffers from gridlock, and there are endemic problems with distribution, partly the result of the government's politically compromised allocation schemes. The resulting shortages have shut down aluminum and steel plants for days and weeks at a time, making it impossible for aspiring businesses to achieve world-class efficiency— and if the business is highly leveraged, putting the entire enterprise at risk or forcing it to issue new equity, thus diluting shareholder value. Some private companies try to secure sources of coal on their own, but most are not equipped to do so, nor did they factor it into their expansion plans five years ago.

Around the world, companies have been looking to secure supplies of key resources by acquiring the production. Vertical integration fell from fashion in recent decades because it is generally less efficient than sticking to the main business, but now it's reviving as a defense mechanism. Borealis, a $9 billion European petrochemical company, linked up with Abu Dhabi National Oil Company to assure access to essential supplies of petroleum feedstock to allow them to grow together in the Asia Pacific region (see Chapter 7 for the full story). Arcelor Mittal, the world's largest steel company (started in Indonesia by Indian-born Lakshmi Mittal and now headquartered in Luxembourg), secured access to iron ore by expanding into mining—a costly bet given that both steelmaking and mining are scale-driven, capital-intensive industries. One Indian power company CEO I know canceled plans to build a plant because his company could not secure a supply of coal. But another, who had moved aggressively into building power plants, simultaneously acquired a mine in Australia as his source of supply. Quoting Jack Welch, the CEO said, "Control your destiny or someone else will."

Technology and talent are less-tangible resources, but they are real components of value creation and competitive advantage that companies often go to great lengths to secure. Again, India provides a clear example. Its engineering schools produce about 400,000 graduates a year. Of these the 125,000 best will be snapped up by the five big IT companies—Infosys, Tata Consultancy Services, Wipro, Satyam, and Cognizant—which have upped the ante in terms of salaries, in-house training programs, and perquisites like food courts. Smaller players in the software sector recruit a further 100,000. This leaves a shrunken pool for manufacturing and all other sectors of the economy. As with any critical input, shortage of talent gives rise to wage increases—for Indian software engineers—of between 10 and 15 percent a year for experienced and specialized professionals. And the quest for talent crosses industries and geographic boundaries. Mining companies from South Africa, Indonesia, Australia, and Brazil are luring Indian engineering grads, offering them three times more than Indian companies can pay.[30] Companies improve their choice of candidates by building a reputation for great work conditions and fast-track careers, but the challenge is ongoing.

Water shortages are becoming serious in Asia, the Middle East, and North Africa. People with more money eat better; protein-rich foods like chicken and beef require much more water to produce than a similar quantity of grain. For example, China's water supplies are increasingly constrained by overexploitation and pollution. Moreover, water from melting Himalayan glaciers flows through China, to Nepal, Bangladesh, and India via the Brahmaputra and Ganges rivers. Some two-thirds of it is used for agriculture in northern India, which feeds much of the rest of the country. But China has been building dams upstream, which can reduce that flow considerably. China is India's largest trading partner, and India has a trade deficit with China to the tune of $40 billion with no reversal in sight. It doesn't take a lot of imagination to consider how China's economic power might spill into negotiations over water, hurting individuals, businesses, and India as a whole. Would smaller countries similarly affected, such as Vietnam and Cambodia and other members of the Association of Southeast Asian Nations, join together to gain influence? These possibilities should enter your mind as you look at the external environment.

SORTING THE
ONGOING CHALLENGES

I've defined the major shapers of the tilt from North to South as the global financial system, the new varieties of capitalism, demographics, and digitization. But how do these trends combine? What do they have in common and where might they push in opposite directions? What will change any one of them, and how might that affect the others? You will arrive at your own insights through asking and answering questions.

Start by asking yourself what the unstoppable trends might be. These are major ones that seem highly unlikely to reverse:

- the march toward economic parity of nations and the rise of the middle class
- intensifying competition among countries for jobs and resources
- continuing imbalances in trade and discrepancies in national growth rates
- a shortage of leadership talent and skills in high-growth countries
- continual interconnectedness and disequilibrium in the global financial system

Don't think of this list as definitive. Some trends may be more or less important in your situation—or you may think of others. Choose your own, and tap the brains at your company to test them. One way to do so is to schedule an off-site meeting of your top team and have the group brainstorm what they're observing in the world, and repeat the exercise every quarter. (Any business leader can do this; you don't have to be a CEO.) This is a time for both gathering facts and exercising imagination. As you do, consider a time frame of ten or twenty years, beyond most companies' planning horizons. This will help you break away from the usual assumptions and straight-line projections of the current industry and company plans.

Ask your team to look at what is happening in the world, in various countries, in the industry, and in other industries, and narrow it down to a handful of trends that the group agrees on, making sure there is some internal consistency or logic to them. In other words, what is the team's point of view about where the world is going and why? Then try this: Break the teams into smaller groups and ask each group to consider one of the trends you've identified from the viewpoint of a particular country or region. Let's say you've agreed that China's economic growth will be tepid as smaller Asian countries take over low-cost manufacturing. One team might take the view of China, another of the United States, another of, say, Vietnam. What actions might that country take? What would they mean for your company? For the competition? What could accelerate or reverse that trend? Chances are that some people will gravitate toward the macro view, perhaps focusing on issues of international policy, while others focus on the nitty-gritty. The trick is knitting those things together. Policy issues are relevant to business for two basic reasons: first, because policy directly affects company decisions such as where to locate facilities, where to recruit talent, what markets to enter, and where to raise capital; and second, because businesses can influence policy, as some leaders in the South do through their social networks. CEOs face the choice of whether to accept the externals or try to change them.

Don't stop at the obvious. Dig deeper and consider what chain reactions might get triggered and what might set them off. In forming a broad and long-term view of the externals, you might see that the center of gravity for some industries—possibly your own—is tilting as well, just as machine tools and automobiles shifted to Japan in earlier decades. The South could well dominate telecom ten or twenty years out (note Bharti Airtel's expansion to Africa and China Telecom's partnership with AT&T), and even some R&D-intensive industries such as pharmaceuticals, where India's Ranbaxy is already a global player. (Japan's Daiichi Sankyo bought a majority stake in Ranbaxy in 2009 to shore up its own R&D.) Many companies, even dominant ones, will find themselves on shaky ground as they recognize that their strategy has a limited shelf life or that key markets could shift faster than they'd planned or that their expansion plans bump up against harsh realities of limited resources or talent.

If you accept the trends I've identified, consider the implications not only for your company and your industry but also for the policy makers whose actions will increasingly affect your plans. For example, given the interconnectedness of the global financial system, what mechanisms might arise to coordinate it? In late November 2011, the central banks of the United States, Japan, Canada, the UK, and Switzerland made a coordinated move to ease Europe's liquidity crunch—tacit acknowledgment that they all have a stake in the stability of the global financial system. Will backroom diplomacy give way to a more formal means of protecting the system? If Washington can't rein in Wall Street, will outsiders create pressure for reform? Perhaps creditors of the United States will use foreign ambassadors or representatives to make strong demands.

The greatest risks to the global financial system come through mispricing (as when assets are not sufficiently discounted for risk), lack of liquidity, and concentration or the so-called herd effect. It's possible for a layperson to spot these things at least some of the time—and important because of the connection between risk in the global financial system and the real economy. For example, the bursting of the U.S. housing bubble really should not have been a surprise. The toxic combination of easy money, lax lending standards, incentives for loan officers to crank out mortgages to buyers who couldn't afford them, and the packaging of the resulting shaky loans into triple-A-rated securities was there for all to see. Anyone scrutinizing this combination knowledgeably and thoughtfully could have sketched a pretty good scenario of the outcome. Yet most of the business and financial communities failed to see it coming. The few who were able to lift their heads above the herd belief in growth without end came out of the financial crisis either unscathed or considerably richer.

What might be the signals for a trend that affects your business? Where are the flawed assumptions? What will be the breaking point? For example, are today's imbalances between creditor and debtor nations—China and the United States being Exhibit A—a similar potential source of problems? Foreign institutional investment is usually ahead of the game, so a concentration in its flow can be a sign of trouble down the road. Acceleration can also be a warning sign, for example, when the price of something begins to increase at a faster clip.

Some questions about trends affect almost every global business: If growth continues at a fast pace in Africa, Asia, and Latin America, will the demand for capital outstrip availability? Might sovereign wealth funds become more nationalistic, allowing only domestic investment, giving those countries an advantage? That's a question McKinsey Global Institute raised in its report "Farewell to Cheap Capital?"[31]

It's often argued that inflation is inevitable as countries ease their money supply to spur growth. How will that affect borrowing costs, and what does that say about how much debt you should carry at what maturity? Many Indian and Brazilian companies borrowed in dollars in recent years, counting on steady appreciation of their domestic currencies. When the rupee failed to appreciate and the Brazilian real took an unexpected dip, a good many got in trouble. Such financial missteps can delay competitive moves, leaving ripe opportunities unpicked.

What might various countries do if trade imbalances continue? Could smaller ones such as Vietnam and Thailand form a coalition to counter China's asymmetric power? Will nationalism rise or wane? Will currency wars subside or intensify? Will business behavior win out over political agendas, even in China? China has allowed U.S. companies to buy hundreds of small Chinese firms over the years. Then, in 2011, the government gave Caterpillar permission to acquire a major manufacturer of mining equipment. Is this a sign of change?

Most leaders tend to get absorbed in the volatility of trends, obsessing on their immediate effects on business. What makes a leader exceptional is the mental and psychological ability to cut through the gyrations and keep focused on the big picture.

Not everything will have a neat conclusion, but by thinking through external trends and their implications you'll know what you don't know and therefore what to track. That, in turn, will increase your confidence and decisiveness. Over time you'll build your mental capacity and raise the odds that you'll see what others don't. But you can't wait for all of the pieces to fall into place. While you need to see the big picture, you don't want to miss the narrow window of time in which it's possible to stake out strategic positions and critical resources for the long term. Even in the face of incomplete knowledge, you have to act.

You can start filling the gaps right now as you turn to the next chapter. I'm going to take you inside some tough competitors of the South, the trailblazers who are positioning themselves to become global leaders in their industries. You'll see firsthand their best practices and managerial tools—not to mention the leadership psychology that drives them.

THE GLOBAL FINANCIAL CRISIS:
WHO DEALT THIS MESS?

I've often looked for a short and easy-to-grasp explanation of the crisis's causes, but have found none that do a thorough job. What follows is a concise description of the key factors and players that contributed to it, in the proper sequence. My purpose is to help you understand the workings of the system and its interconnectedness.

LET THE MONEY FLOW

As with many such crises, it began with a flood of easy money. In the aftermath of the dot-com crash in 2000 and the September 11 terrorist attack in 2001, U.S. fiscal and monetary spigots were opened wide to stave off recession. The government cut taxes and raised spending, which increased further when the country went to war. Federal Reserve chairman Alan Greenspan ratcheted down interest rates steadily; by July 2003 they were at 1 percent, the lowest in half a century.

As the markets overflowed with liquidity, Congress and both the Clinton and Bush administrations set out to widen home ownership by directing Fannie Mae (Federal National Mortgage Association) and Freddie Mac (Federal Home Loan Mortgage Corporation) to relax credit standards. The combination of low interest rates and easy loans drove an increase in housing construction and a surge in real estate prices. Private lenders were all too happy to leap on the bandwagon, issuing so-called subprime mortgages that reduced lending standards to the point of irrelevance. Housing became the main driver of the U.S. economy: "By the fall of 2005, Merrill Lynch estimated that half of all U.S. economic growth was related to housing—including new construction, home sales, furniture, and appliances."[32]

Much of the borrowing was by homeowners who refinanced and spent the money on everything from cars and clothing to vacations, helping to sustain consumption in the face of falling real wages. Their urge to splurge was further underwritten by the rising stock market, which made many of them richer—on paper. Indeed, you could say that the housing bubble was one aspect of a much larger phenomenon—let's call it a confidence bubble: Things were great and could only get better! Household debt roughly doubled from 2000 to 2008, to almost $14 trillion,[33] helping to raise the U.S. trade deficit to a peak of $763.3 billion in 2006. The main beneficiaries of the spending: China and oil-exporting nations. Both acquired enormous foreign reserves.

The vast amounts of money pumped into the system helped drive a worldwide economic boom that pushed up the prices of natural resources and created housing bubbles in other countries. Oil prices, denominated in dollars, rose as the dollar weakened; they spiked to nearly $100 a barrel in 2008, their highest level ever. The Fed actually raised rates from 2004 through 2006, but to little effect: money came pouring in from overseas as investors from Berlin to Beijing lent their savings to credit-crazed Americans.

THE MARKETS KNOW BEST

The circus that preceded the meltdown was made possible only by the erosion of regulations that had governed the financial markets for decades. (A high point was the repeal of the Glass-Steagall Act of 1933, which had created a firewall between commercial banks and investment banks.) Deregulation was spurred by a Congress responding to the urgings of the financial community, and it was blessed by Greenspan—an ardent champion of free markets—as a wellspring of healthy financial innovation.

One decision by the Securities and Exchange Commission was key; it allowed major Wall Street firms such as Goldman Sachs, Morgan Stanley, Lehman Brothers, Bear Stearns, and Merrill Lynch to exceed the long-standing limit on their debt-to-net-capital ratio of 12:1. The decision allowed them to up their leverage to as much as 40:1, raising stupendous amounts of high-risk money leveraged on short-term funds from banks and money-market funds. (It is no coincidence that three of the five firms are now history.) They invested much of it in collateralized debt obligations (CDOs) comprised of those shaky mortgages. The risk ended up far from its creators, in the hands of mostly uninformed customers looking for high returns. Executive compensation linked to the soaring stock prices of these firms inspired lenders to push homeowner borrowing still more, often with shoddy practices and to people who couldn't afford the mortgages.

THEY CALL THEM SECURITIES?

Among other things, deregulation allowed the creation of exotic debt instruments, most notably CDOs and credit default swaps, which were to play a major role in the debacle. CDOs were highly complex securities—so complex that even those who created and sold them often did not understand them—through which lenders took loans off their balance sheets and sold them in bundles to investors. Credit default swaps were a form of insurance designed to protect institutional buyers against defaults.

The CDOs were based on proprietary mathematical models for trading, designed by a small number of PhDs whose specialties are mathematics and physics. The content of those black boxes was a mystery to others, including almost all the firms' senior-level leadership and boards of directors. In the run-up to 2008, anybody who cared to know what was going on had to rely mostly on supervisors several levels below the CEO who oversaw the specialists and traders.

Among the clueless were S&P, Moody's, and Fitch, the major ratings agencies. They continued to classify many potentially toxic securities as AAA. At the time, only twelve companies in the world carried this top rating—yet sixty-four thousand securitization packages received it.

No wonder Warren Buffett famously—and presciently—called those instruments "weapons of financial mass destruction." The breakdown of the system was only a matter of time. Surprisingly, the decision to allow greater leverage was made when the SEC was under the chairmanship of Bill Donaldson, a cofounder of Donaldson, Lufkin & Jenrette (DLJ), whose expertise and experience should have given him the foundation for understanding the implications of such a move. That is, when a financial institution is on the ropes and confidence in it fades, leverage works faster and more effectively in reverse. The chain reaction can—and did—swiftly bring the system to a halt.

THE LEVERS KICK BACK

That's what happened when Lehman Brothers went under. Lehman had huge and heavily leveraged investments in subprime mortgage securities, and investors were—at long last—starting to realize how insecure they were. Throughout 2008 Lehman's holdings were deflating at an accelerated rate, and the firm was hemorrhaging money. It began frantically looking for a buyer, but couldn't strike a deal, and the U.S. Treasury declined to bail it out.

When Lehman filed for bankruptcy on September 15, the already battered Dow Jones fell some 500 points, its largest single-day drop since the aftermath of 9/11. But that wasn't the worst of the fallout. One of the oldest and biggest players in the $2.6 trillion money market fund industry, the Reserve Primary Fund, had invested some $785 million in Lehman debt securities. These became essentially worthless with the bankruptcy, and drove the Reserve Fund's net asset value below the $1 per share that money market funds customarily maintained—an event called "breaking the buck." Reserve was forced to suspend redemptions to investors—a cataclysmic breach of faith in an industry whose products were considered second only to banks in their safety.

Next to fall were the so-called monoline insurers that guaranteed payments on all manner of bonds, including municipals. They had insured trillions of dollars' worth of CDOs (which not incidentally acquired the insurers' AAA ratings as a result). Leveraged as they were, few were able to pay out when those securities suddenly lost a significant amount of their value. Some 80 percent of this business was concentrated in one firm, AIG, which dominated the market for credit default swaps.

THE RECKONING ON MAIN STREET

It's a simple but often forgotten fact that confidence is the underpinning of any financial system; without it, none of the players can function.

The ensuing destruction of confidence began in the United States but spread almost instantly through the highly interconnected world financial system. There was panic in some quarters, and emergency meetings around the globe. Worldwide financial collapse seemed a real possibility. Frightened investors pulled their money out of just about anything in sight. Stock markets plunged, and margin calls further squeezed liquidity as buyers disappeared. Falling stock prices demolished corporate debt ratings and ravaged retirement funds. Forced to pull cash out of operations, businesses contracted and economies fell into a fast downward spiral. The misery spread quickly to Main Street as hundreds of thousands of jobs vanished, and a growing number of people could no longer afford to pay their mortgages. Municipal bond markets dried up, depriving governments of the funding they needed to operate and build. Mortgage lenders hoping to salvage their loans—vainly, as it turned out—began massive and often brutal foreclosures.

It might have been the Great Depression redux had not U.S. policymakers pulled together the massive intervention that included the celebrated bailouts and TARP rescue fund. The fierce political controversy the programs generated should not be allowed to dim the magnitude of the accomplishments: Without those actions, it's hard to imagine what could have prevented a global financial collapse. As it is, the United States and many other nations have been left suffering from high unemployment and weighed down by debt, and they are not expected to fully recover for years.

CHAPTER THREE

THE NEW POWER OF THE SOUTH

T he vast possibilities created by the tilt may seem hard to imagine to leaders who've spent their careers in the North. Their counterparts in the South have no reservations. Opportunities of a lifetime are suddenly right in their own backyards, igniting their passion and fueling the very fast growth of business empires that will cast shadows on the North for decades. Think of the nineteenth-century United States: The exuberant growth of this young industrial nation, with its boundless opportunities, produced such iconic titans as Cornelius Vanderbilt, J. P. Morgan, Andrew Carnegie, and John D. Rockefeller. Their towering enterprises dominated the world economic scene for decades. Today the beckoning landscape is in the South, and the empire builders have been born and raised in countries such as India, China, Brazil, South Africa, and Malaysia. They are especially well equipped to seize big opportunities, not just because of where they live but also because of who they are—a potent mix of ambition, tenacity, and business savvy, often shaped by conditions of hardship and scarcity.

Take, for example, India, my home country, where families have been businesspeople for generations and training begins early in school and at home. From a young age children learn to do calculations in their heads, starting with multiplication tables and progressing to increasingly large numbers and more complex calculations. At home around the dinner table, they are immersed in discussions of cash, margins, revenue, debt, and capital—the elements of business acumen. The younger people listen and absorb. I distinctly recall my own family members, who ran a shoe shop, discussing how to handle cash when collections from customers were slow because of the monsoon. In India, business activity is clustered around four cultural groups—the Marwaris, Gujaratis, Parsis, and Bania—largely in the states of Uttar Pradesh and Rajasthan, Gujarat, and Maharashtra. The products of this culture include such luminaries as Sunil Mittal of Bharti Airtel, whom we met in the first chapter, Lakshmi and Aditya Mittal of the global ArcelorMittal steel empire, Aditya Vikram Birla and Kumar Mangalam Birla of the AV Birla Group (now India's third-largest industrial company), Dhirubhai Ambani and Mukesh Ambani of Reliance Industries,

J. R. D. Tata of Tata Group, and many other less-well-known but extraordinarily successful business leaders.

Other countries in the South have their own versions of these large-scale entrepreneurs, as I call them, with the same kind of ambition, tenacity, and business acumen. Facing opportunities they never even dreamed of, their energy is bursting forth like oil from a newly drilled well. They are growing small businesses into big ones, expanding beyond their home countries and continents, entering entirely new kinds of businesses, making acquisitions, and overtaking entrenched competitors, all at a dazzling pace. An American company might think 4 percent revenue growth is acceptable; a Southern company thinks 20 percent is normal.

The companies of the South often seek the advice of investment bankers and consultants, many from the North, to identify the best opportunities, and they use partnerships, joint ventures, licensing deals, and acquisitions—whatever it takes—to establish themselves in a market or industry and scale up quickly. Because their companies are young, they're not hamstrung by bureaucracy, so they move fast. Often the best opportunities are in niches or geographic markets that are on the periphery. They use those wins to learn and build strength as they focus on the bigger target: overtaking entrenched multinationals and winning in the global game. They hire the best operational executives they can find, people with great track records who know the business and their domain as well as or better than anyone in the world, and give them authority to make decisions. They woo them with the excitement of very fast growth and attractive compensation. High salaries for the right people are almost a rounding error compared with quantum increases in the market caps of their companies.

Tata Motors' selection of leaders to run the luxury-car business it acquired from Ford Motor Company is representative of the approach to talent I've seen in many companies of the South. In 2008 it was making four million vehicles a year, primarily trucks and small cars. Its leaders had no experience in the luxury-car segment when it bought Jaguar and Land Rover (JLR) from Ford for $2.3 billion that year. It filled the void by hiring people who had that expertise. As growth returned after the global financial crisis, Tata hired Ralf Speth, who had spent most of his career at BMW, to run JLR. Given Speth's deep knowledge of the luxury-car market, there wasn't much of a learning curve. He quickly analyzed how to position JLR to benefit from the economic recovery, for example, by expanding the range of products to meet Mercedes and BMW's fuller lines, something Ford had not done because of financial constraints. Under his direction, JLR produced, among other things, the new Range Rover Evoque (designed by Ford), which was named *Motor Trend*'s SUV of the year in 2012. And in the spring of that year JLR was on track for record-breaking pretax profits and seeking space to expand production in the UK. Its incredible technology and know-how in engineering and design have put Tata Motors on a whole new trajectory globally.

Many Southern leaders are also remarkably good at execution. A lifetime of scarcity and tight margins has taught them discipline. They can cut through the numbers to detect and diagnose the root causes of performance and link those results with people. The causal factor could be an individual or the indecisiveness of a group—say, in making joint decisions. It could be a person who left and didn't get replaced. They aren't satisfied until they know what actually drives the numbers. Funding growth is not a problem for them either. Investors in the South flock to companies that are determined to win in high-growth markets and have a track record in execution. Leaders of the South also are accustomed to the vagaries of the government and regulators and to the inadequacies of ubiquities such as electrical power.

These are the companies the North is now competing with not only for markets but also for capital and talent. Leaders in the North who ignore these players may suddenly discover that they are far behind in many markets that were once insignificant but are now on fire. This chapter provides examples of Southern companies that are well on their way to being number one or two in the world and in some cases are able to swallow companies with hefty market shares and well-known brands, the purpose being to convince you that this competition is real, unrelenting, and based on excellence in leadership, strategy, and execution, not some fleeting advantage in cost or currency. This is what you need to know about your new competitors.

THEY'RE EXPERT AT LEARNING NEW BUSINESSES: GMR GROUP

India's GMR Group is a prime example of what I call large-scale entrepreneurs (LSEs). The South today—particularly India, Indonesia, Malaysia, and Singapore—is turning them out by the dozens. These would-be empire builders make big strategic bets and quickly build very large businesses based on the opportunity they see rather than the core competence they possess. They pick the fast-growing markets they want to be in and build the capabilities they need to succeed in them, even if they are starting with zero experience.

They manage for cash, and may take low margins for sustained periods to create scale, coverage, and brand strength. While those low margins pose the risk of liquidity crunches, they can build long-term economic value and sustain short-term blows as long as they have better cost structures than their competitors, and continue to build consumer interest. You will be competing with these savvy operators not only for markets but also for talent: they're looking for it wherever they can find it, and they are attractive employers for good executives whose careers have been advancing slowly in low-growth Northern companies.

These leaders have not only the optimism, tenacity, and drive that lone-wolf entrepreneurs possess, but also superb business acumen: an obsession with exactly how money will be made and under what conditions, which enables them to attract financing. They know how to choose people with top-notch operating skills who can quickly build teams to execute the specifics of strategy. They are comfortable working with tight margins, and they are patient: they build for the long-term. All of this is undergirded by self-confidence earned through previous success and boundless ambition. With each new win, they build confidence to pursue the next big opportunity.

A $10 billion global company based in Bangalore and the largest infrastructure company in India, GMR owns more than a hundred businesses directly or through holding companies. These range from power generation and highways to real estate, sports franchises, and security services. Founder G. M. Rao and his family own 70 percent of the publicly traded company; Rao continues to run the company, and his two sons and one son-in-law are sector directors, overseeing major operating units comprising dozens of infrastructure projects and joint ventures, many on a huge scale and some now outside of India in places such as Turkey, Singapore, and the Maldives.

The story of how GMR came to dominate India's infrastructure business reveals large-scale entrepreneurship in action. Because much of its business is with India's public sector, the company has been hurt lately by the fickle and often irrational policies of the Indian national and state governments. But GMR's leaders have the resilience to keep moving ahead, and the long time horizon that comes with family control: they are highly conscious of building for their future generations.

I grew up in a village thirty-six miles from Delhi and earned my undergraduate degree from Banaras University, some three hundred miles away. As recently as the early 1980s, when I returned to India to visit family and attend events at my alma mater, the trip from my home to Banaras took about forty hours by train. Neither was there a coordinated road system to speak of: It took five days for a truck to drive the thousand miles from Delhi to Kolkata. India's highway infrastructure was as undeveloped as its government-owned airports, power grid, seaports, and communications network.

Inefficiency and limited resources meant that millions of people were off the power grid, airports were shabby and overcrowded, and road travel was arduous or, in the rainy season, impossible. In the mid-1990s, as India began to liberalize the tight rules governing economic activity under the so-called License Raj system, in which all economic activity was license based, the Indian government pledged to invest billions of dollars in its infrastructure. But even that amount wouldn't fill the void. To supplement it, the political leaders opened the door for private parties to invest their own money building ports, highways, power-generating plants, telecom systems, and airports fit for a modern country. While India's infrastructure is still grossly inadequate, it has come a long way since the 1990s: mobile phones are now in the hands of some 269 million people; 3,600 miles of highway have been built as part of India's Golden Quadrilateral project connecting the cities of Delhi, Mumbai, Chennai, and Kolkata; 4,000 megawatts of electrical power capacity have been added to the grid; and the international airports of Mumbai, Delhi, Hyderabad, and Bangalore have been upgraded.

GMR would not have participated in that growth if it hadn't been for Rao's willingness to take chances, learn fast, and execute well—and his ability to instill all of that in the company as it expanded. Investors, including Temasek Investments from Singapore in the energy business and Macquarie of Australia, have been won over. They are in it for the longer time horizon that infrastructure demands, typically seven to ten years, earning rates of return in the mid-teens. Trained as a mechanical engineer in Andhra Pradesh, Rao started his career in a jute mill and gradually expanded his reach into other businesses, including brewing, banking, and insurance. He was in his forties when liberalization began in earnest, and he saw infrastructure as an opportunity and a social good on a much bigger scale. His entrepreneurial instincts drew him to it. Companies in the South don't usually start out with the reams of data that precede the launch of a new venture in the North—the data either don't exist or are too aggregate to be useful, and there's no market research department to drill down further. So there's a lot of learning as you go, the success of which depends crucially on intuition, judgment, the ability to pinpoint a small number of key variables, and relationship-building capabilities with multiple governments, regulators, and potential partners.

Rao's first opportunity to venture into infrastructure came in 1995, when the Indian government opened to the private sector bidding to build a power-generation plant in the state of Tamil Nadu. GMR had never built a power plant, but it was willing to take the project on. It submitted a bid and won, then sought the expertise to do it. Rao turned to K. V. V. Rao, a former classmate from Andhra University. He had great technical knowledge and was detail oriented. But could he oversee the design and construction of a power plant—something he had never done? Trusting his own ability to select the right person, G. M. Rao bet—correctly—that his former classmate would rise to the challenge.

Power plants, like all infrastructure projects, represent a major commitment of human energy and resources for typically five years and in some cases considerably more, from planning to operation. Contractors and subcontractors are involved, as are several governments at almost every step, especially when the plant goes online. That's when GMR would begin selling its output to the state electricity board that bought and distributed it and the municipality that controlled the tariffs, or pricing. GMR navigated all of this, hiring some people from the public sector to ensure that the project met the government's requirements. That experience emboldened GMR to build two more power plants in neighboring states in the next few years, with equal success.

When opportunities arose in highway construction, GMR again jumped in, despite the fact that it had never built a road. The government was seeking bidders to not only lay the all-weather pavement but also operate and maintain it. GMR partnered with a Malaysian road-building entity for the first project and with another experienced player for the second. As in power-plant construction, GMR learned the business fast and succeeded. It was on its own for a third road-construction project.

GMR's appetite grew in step with its successes in infrastructure. Given the enormity of opportunities not just in India but worldwide, it created better guidelines for choosing which areas to pursue. "Coming specifically to the airport business, we had no understanding of this sector," says Kumar Mangalam Birla. "But we did have a set of data that made us comfortable. We found a study that showed the market capitalization for top companies in the airline and airports business. Nine of the top ten market capitalizations were in airports. Just one was an airline. From that data we knew that the opportunities were big. It was enough to convince us to really go aggressive into the airport business, even though we had no idea about it."[1] Having grasped the size of the long-term opportunity, Rao and Kumar set about making it happen.

When construction of the new Greenfield International Airport at Hyderabad was coming up for bid, GMR saw its chance. Since it couldn't even meet the qualifying criteria to enter a bid, it turned to Malaysia Airports Holdings Berhad, a publicly traded company that operated and maintained thirty-nine airports in Malaysia, which lent its expertise for a fee. The Indian government wanted firmer involvement from an experienced player, so Rao spent time convincing the Malaysians to make a financial commitment. It was not a case of instant bonding. The Malaysians had a dim view of India's intent to modernize and weren't sure they wanted to get involved. Rao eventually boosted their confidence in GMR, and they took a 10 percent equity stake in the new venture. With that, GMR submitted a bid to construct from scratch a $600 million, twelve-million-passenger airport. The bid had to cover everything from initial design to commissioning, at which point the airport would be open for business. GMR focused on the details and won the bid.

The company had to continue learning about airports and at the same time execute the project. The schedule didn't allow for one to precede the other. Ongoing dialogue helped accomplish both. Kumar held a rigorous daylong review every Monday to bring alignment among the team members who'd been pulled together from other companies, organizations, and countries—alignment in the way they thought, the way they acted, and, Kumar adds, the way they felt. Once a month, his father conducted a similar review.

Initially, Kumar's reviews were a quick update on what each department was doing. Later, department heads presented what new actions or initiatives they were undertaking. Gradually, the emphasis shifted to a fifty-fifty balance between monitoring and learning. Meeting commitments was always front and center, reflecting the constants of scarcity and tight margins in India. Learning took many forms. For example, the team would discuss what others were doing about retail formats or fueling or cargo, sometimes prompting further study of best practices in Hong Kong or Singapore. When differences of opinion surfaced, they increasingly got resolved among the team rather than being passed up to Kumar.

The Hyderabad airport project was a success, and GMR soon had a chance to apply its newfound learning about airports when it bid to construct new airports in Delhi and Mumbai in 2005. The stakes were higher this time. The project was high profile and potentially highly profitable. Competition from experienced players was intense.

GMR took on two operating partners, Malaysian Airports Holdings Berhad and Frankfort Airport Services Worldwide, each of which had a 10 percent stake in the airport venture. It took around eighteen months, seventy-five full-time people, and close to $10 million just to prepare the bid. But GMR overcame its relative inexperience and lack of close ties with top government officials by focusing on what it could do better than others. That led to an intense focus on the technical aspects of the plan. When bids are evaluated, they receive "points" for meeting specific criteria. GMR worked hard to meet them and was the only company to receive eighty-five points. It won the bid, which allowed it to choose between the two airports. It chose Delhi.

The Indira Gandhi International Airport in Delhi was built in just thirty-seven months and opened on July 3, 2010, to rave reviews. A shiny glass-and-steel structure that sprawls over an area of 5.4 million square feet, the new terminal is the world's sixth largest, with seventy-eight aerobridges connecting planes to the terminal, 168 check-in counters, multiple lounges and shower rooms, twenty thousand square meters of commercial space, and air-conditioned parking for more than four thousand cars. Prime Minister Manmohan Singh said that it signaled the arrival of "new India" and "proves the success of the Public-Private Partnership model in execution of large infrastructure projects." Civil Aviation Minister Praful Patel praised GMR for completing the project in record time, noting that GMR Group was much sought after for international projects—clear testament to GMR's success in a business it built from scratch and to the opportunities that now lay at its feet.

In each new area GMR ventures into, it takes command, learns fast, and executes well. In airports, the team learned from service providers, cargo companies, duty-free operators, vendors, architects around the world, along with conferences and extensive reading. The ability to learn a new area is deeply embedded in the company's DNA. "I've learned it from my father," Kumar asserts. "Whenever he meets a new person he spends half the time learning about that person. All through my childhood I observed him interacting with other people in this way. He was constantly gathering information, whether it was from a junior employee or a senior person or a government leader." Kumar himself interviews the senior people who join the company to learn how their former companies run the business.

GMR now takes its expertise in airports beyond India. It won the bid to develop an international airport in Istanbul, Turkey, for example, and completed a project to expand the Maldives' Ibrahim Nasir International Airport four months ahead of schedule. (In late 2012 a new political regime canceled GMR's contract to also run it.)

Doing something untried continues to be a company-wide passion, and GMR is on the watch for more large-scale opportunities in areas it may not know anything about. It still allows for "gut feeling" in spotting the opportunities. Kumar explains, "When you travel a lot and meet different people in government and industry, you understand what the gaps are. Once you interact at the ground level, you can tell whether the opportunity is right, and then you can look more closely at it. Today we have huge migration from rural to urban, and cities are getting congested, so we are exploring opportunities in urban infrastructure."

THEY CAN BUY THEIR WAY INTO THE BIG LEAGUES: HINDALCO INDUSTRIES

Northern companies can come under pressure to divest divisions that aren't pulling their weight. The business may be poorly managed, or shareholders might be pressing for short-term earnings at the expense of investment that could build the business up over the long term. These are ripe opportunities for globally ambitious leaders to acquire them, integrate them quickly, take corrective action, and use them to further the goal of being number one or two in the world. Leaders can use them as platforms not only to get a foothold in the North, but also to build markets in other Southern countries and prevent a Northern competitor from penetrating their territories. They don't overwhelm the acquisition with tons of overseers sent from their home country. Instead they assign a few select high-level people who are carefully picked for their ability to fix operational problems.

A case in point is Hindalco, an aluminum company that is part of one of India's largest entities, Aditya Birla Group. From its base in India, Hindalco has come to dominate the aluminum industry, helped by its deft handling of Novelis, a division of the Canadian company Alcan that was four times larger than Hindalco when it was acquired in 2007. (Note that I am on Hindalco's board of directors.)

When Kumar Mangalam Birla took over Aditya Birla Group in 1995, the company was one of India's largest, with $2 billion in revenues. But none of its businesses was globally dominant, and that spelled opportunity to the great-grandson of the founder. Educated in India and at the London Business School, he had been propelled suddenly into Birla's top job at the age of twenty-eight after the untimely death of his father, and many observers doubted that he could successfully lead the group, with its diverse mix of businesses ranging from aluminum and cement to fertilizers, textiles, and clothing. As things turned out, he has led it splendidly.

The company has its roots in cotton trading in the nineteenth century and has been led by succeeding generations of family members ever since, who have added, among other businesses, Grasim (a fiber, cement, and chemical company) and Hindalco. Aditya Vikram Birla, Kumar's father, entered the business in the late 1960s as a young man with an MIT engineering degree and an entrepreneur's drive that went beyond the family business he had inherited. While successfully running the family company, he started businesses from scratch and acquired others, including Indo-Thai Synthetics, which was Birla's first international venture. And there were others: an edible-oils company in Malaysia and a carbon-black company in Thailand (carbon black is used in products such as tires, inks, and plastics).

Following family tradition, the fourth-generation Kumar Mangalam Birla continued to expand into new businesses, among them retail, life insurance, mobile phones, and asset management. But the main challenge he faced early in his tenure was to figure out which businesses to grow and how to fund that growth. The answer lay in operational efficiency, a refocused business portfolio that allowed the company to generate lots of cash, and a plan to use that cash to fund aggressive expansion of its core commodities businesses, primarily aluminum, copper, cement, and fertilizer. Kumar's view of the global landscape had convinced him that worldwide demand would grow and prices would continue to rise. Knowing that scale is a huge determinant of competitiveness in those markets, he set out to achieve it fast by investing $4 billion (Rs 20,000 crore) over four years, focusing on aluminum.

While Hindalco was a dominant player in aluminum in India, it wasn't nearly big enough to compete against global giants such as Alcoa and Alcan. Kumar encouraged Debu Bhattacharya, the managing director put in charge of Hindalco in 2003, to create a blueprint for a giant step. Bhattacharya drew up a plan to invest more in the near term than the group had invested over the previous two decades to build new plants and acquire other companies.

Hindalco was mainly an "upstream" company, mining bauxite and converting it into aluminum. Hindalco CEO Bhattacharya aimed to make it a globally competitive integrated company, as Alcoa and Alcan were, meaning it would also participate in the "downstream" activities of rolling aluminum flat and turning it into marketable products such as Coke cans and car fenders. This would balance the cyclicality and profitability of the upstream world with that of the downstream, where moneymaking was quite different: Upstream activities are more volatile but more profitable; downstream activities are less profitable but less volatile. The upstream and downstream worlds also required different capabilities. Success in mining and production depended heavily on low-cost production and scale. Success in aluminum products, on the other hand, required technological innovation and close ties with customers.

As Hindalco was making its assessment of the global aluminum market, on the other side of the world trouble was brewing for Canada-based Alcan. In 2004 it was in talks to buy a French company but had to divest part of its business to clear the deal with Canadian regulators. Alcan wrapped its $7.8 billion rolled-aluminum business and nearly $2.4 billion in debt into a new entity called Novelis and in 2005 spun it off as an independent company. Despite wobbly financial results, Novelis retained its status as the world's leading producer of rolled aluminum products.

Novelis had just the technological capability and customer relationships Hindalco lacked. It was, however, four times bigger than Hindalco. It took vision and drive—not to mention chutzpah—to pursue the biggest target in AV Birla Group's history and the second-biggest cross-border acquisition ever by any Indian company. The promise was that Hindalco would instantly possess the scale and capabilities to catapult its rank in the global aluminum game. The risk was that the acquisition would be financially ruinous.

In 2006 the company approached Novelis, which put the Canadian company into play. As other bidders showed interest, the price rose and Hindalco backed off. In the meantime, Novelis began to sputter, and other suitors disappeared. Hindalco returned with a $6 billion offer—$3.5 billion in cash and $2.5 billion in the form of assumed debt—and the deal was completed in 2007. The bold move raised more than a few eyebrows, not just because of Hindalco's relative size. Some critics thought the price tag was too high, especially given Novelis's weakness in pricing power. It was locked into contracts that kept prices steady while material costs were rising sharply. Other critics suggested that Hindalco's estimates of demand growth were too rosy. But young Kumar Birla was unfazed. As a large-scale entrepreneur, he was focused on the longer term, when customer contracts would reach their expiration dates and the global economy would get its land legs and take off. He got a lot of advice from trusted experts and advisers not to buy it, but he went ahead.

The acquisition turbo-boosted Birla's status in the global aluminum market, but the parent company was intent on securing and improving that position. Hindalco took Novelis into the fold with great care and respect for its technical expertise and customer relations. Only when it saw that its own expertise in logistics outshone Novelis's did it send people from India to North America. The need for efficiency in the global footprint, combined with top management's view of global demand, spurred decisions about which plants to close and which to expand, including the decision to manufacture some rolled aluminum in India, exporting 20 percent or so until Indian demand caught up.

The parent also set the financial expectations: Hindalco ran a tight ship and expected Novelis to do the same. When results failed to materialize in the early quarters, the parent company didn't let it slide. In 2009 Kumar Mangalam Birla and Bhattacharya recruited Phil Martens as president and chief operating officer. Martens had a solid track record at Ford and at auto parts supplier ArvinMeritor and had a big hand in turning Mazda around in Japan. His skill and speed in taking hold of operations so impressed leaders at Birla that Kumar Mangalam Birla asked him to take the top job, saying in the press release, "[Mr. Martens] has driven the Novelis team from the front, energizing them and raising the bar of the organization in every way."

Novelis has performed well under Martens's leadership and is poised for continued growth. It reported $11 billion in sales and $63 million in profits for fiscal year 2012, and in November 2012 broke ground on its first aluminum plant in China. It is now the world's largest rolled-aluminum company and Asia's largest producer of aluminum not yet made into products. While ensuring that Novelis was meeting performance expectations and positioning for the long term, neither Birla nor Hindalco has felt the need to make Novelis into an Indian company. It is being led by an American CEO with its North American headquarters and R&D facility in Atlanta, yet it is in line with Birla's broad view and long-term ambitions.

THEY CAN WIN BY ENCIRCLING DOMINANT PLAYERS: AB INBEV

Anheuser-Busch dominated the U.S. beer industry for the better part of the twentieth century. Four generations of the Busch family built it aggressively—sometimes ruthlessly—into a powerhouse of distribution, marketing, and branding matched in few industries. In the mid-1990s it had almost half of the U.S. beer market and was one of America's largest owners and operators of theme parks. The Busches were empire builders and the royalty of American brewers. As the twenty-first century arrived and the pace of business globalization accelerated, Anheuser-Busch—with its huge financial resources and a brand known around the world—was in a perfect position to pursue world dominance.

In 2010 the CEO explained what was coming next. "Our business is all about building brands," he said.[2] Those included local and regional brands, each with a distinct heritage and cadre of loyal consumers, and global brands like Budweiser, Stella Artois, and Beck's. Budweiser stood out as what he called "our flagship global brand." Already the number one premium brand in the United States, China, and Canada, it was growing in the UK and other markets and soon to be launched in Russia, Brazil, and Argentina. "Little by little," he promised, "we will take Budweiser to where it belongs, which is the global stage."

The CEO in question, however, is not a Busch, nor any other American. He's the Brazilian empire builder Carlos Brito. The company he heads is AB InBev—the product of the former InBev's acquisition of Anheuser Bush in 2008 and now the world's largest brewer. His story is a vivid example of how a Southern company can overtake a financially healthy but complacent number one in the North.

InBev and many other companies with the same drive thrust themselves onto the global stage through a strategy I call encircling. It's the business version of Mao's strategy for winning in China: first focus on the countryside, then encircle and conquer the cities. It's the same strategy Sam Walton used to build Walmart from a single store in Rogers, Arkansas, to the behemoth that mauled Montgomery Ward, Sears, Kmart, and other giants of their time. By the time they awakened from their naps, the agile enemy was battering down the city gates. The encirclers of the global tilt may start small, but they think big; many aim to ultimately be the number one or number two global player in their industry.

While Anheuser-Busch focused on incremental gains, lulled by its unbeatable market share and brand position in the world's largest market, it failed to notice how it had been encircled. The tip-off could have been South African Breweries' (SAB's) 2002 acquisition of Miller, the second-largest player in America, but if AB noticed, it did not react. Meanwhile, InBev's predecessor, the Brazilian brewer AmBev, was playing serious hardball in the global game of consolidation, pursuing a strategy of cost-cutting and astute financial management.

The aggressively expansionist brewer was backed by three of Brazil's wealthiest investors, Jorge Paulo Lemann, Marcel Herrmann Telles, and Carlos Alberto da Veiga Sicupira, founders of the 3G Capital investment firm. They had engineered the merger of two large Brazilian brewers into AmBev, and continued to expand the company in South America. Brito rose smartly in AmBev through finance, operations, and sales, sharpening his skills in both cost-cutting and finance and proving himself and his team as creators of shareholder value with methodologies that were transportable elsewhere. Made CEO in 2004, he acquired several more companies outside Brazil, further enhancing his credibility with the capital markets, in each case paying back excessive debt within two years to bring the balance sheet in line and increase the earning power of the acquired company.

Brito continued to expand its market capitalization; combined with a strong balance sheet, this positioned him to swallow larger prey. Later that year AmBev sold itself to Interbrew, a Belgian brewer that had also grown rapidly through acquisitions. Within a year, the company—renamed InBev—made Brito its CEO. His ability to raise cash continued to be impeccable. Once again he was able to reduce debt and increase InBev's market cap and earnings power, thereby making a quantum jump. When he went after Anheuser-Busch, the family fought back furiously, but it didn't stand a chance in the face of Brito's moneymaking machine.

AB InBev has been losing market share in the United States since the takeover, amid widespread consumer complaints that cost-cutting has compromised the taste of some beers, including former imports now brewed in America. Company officials dismiss the complaints, but if the perceptions continue to grow, Brita may have to put some costs back in.

Still, the lesson remains. Like so many other established corporations, Anheuser's managers didn't see the power that overseas competitors were amassing. They lost the vision, drive, and boldness that had built their business. Those qualities are more likely to be found today in companies—mostly from the South—that American leaders never paid attention to until they themselves suddenly fell prey to them.

THEY CAN WIN BY AIMING HIGHER: HAIER GROUP

Southern manufacturers typically attack Northern markets with low prices. China's Haier Group is a notable exception: CEO Zhang Ruimin set out to create a global brand that would position his company in the middle and higher ranges. Zhang built his brand by offering high quality, innovation, and impeccable service that could command a premium price. The strategy has paid off handsomely. A weak also-ran in the Chinese market in the early 1980s, Haier has grown to be the world's largest maker of white goods (large appliances). He achieved large global scale by confronting well-established manufacturers of the North on their own territory, and using his success there as leverage to win in the South.

Zhang set this course early in his twenty-eight-year career as Haier's head, when the company was still exporting its goods from China. "The objective of most Chinese enterprises is to export products and earn foreign currency," he told Harvard Business School researchers back then. "This is their only purpose. Our purpose in exporting is to establish a brand reputation."[3]

The strategy was an extension of Haier's heritage. The company began life as a nearly bankrupt municipally owned refrigerator company in Qingdao. Like other Chinese appliances, the refrigerators were cheap and poorly made. Zhang, whom the government had put in charge of the ailing business in 1984, believed that consumers would be glad to pay more for higher quality and reliable service. But how could he deliver these in a country with little tradition of first-class consumer goods manufacturing? A trip to Germany provided his answer, and he signed a technology licensing agreement with refrigerator maker Liebherr. To make sure the technology translated into salable products, Zhang drilled the then-unfamiliar concept of quality into his workers. At one point, for example, he pulled seventy-six refrigerators off the line, some for minor flaws such as scratches, and ordered staff to smash them to bits. "That got their attention," laughed Zhang. "They finally understood that I wasn't going to sell just anything, like my competitors would. It had to be the best."

Haier turned a profit in Zhang's second year and went on to win a gold medal for quality in a 1988 national competition. The timing was perfect. The refrigerator market had become glutted, and competitors were cutting their prices. Zhang, however, raised his prices 15 percent, banking—correctly—on his notion that people would pay for quality. He also found opportunity in the abysmal service provided by other Chinese producers. For example, when refrigerators broke down, which they did frequently, customers would have to wait weeks for repairs. Haier not only built more reliable machines, but it fixed the ones that did fail faster and lent consumers replacements in the meantime. By the end of 1989, when revenues had grown more than tenfold to 410 million renminbi, the company had built a computerized service center and was starting to build a network of service contractors. In the early 1990s, Zhang scaled up, building a thoroughly up-to-date new plant from which Haier did contract manufacturing for original equipment manufacturers while selling an expanding range of its own appliances. Leveraging its operational and service expertise, Haier also grew by buying underperforming Chinese appliance makers and turning them around. He targeted firms with good products but bad management, then fixed them. For example, in 1995 the Qingdao municipal government urged Haier to buy a failing washing machine company. In a year and a half, Haier took the business from near bankruptcy to being the top-rated washing machine manufacturer in China. By that time, Haier was also China's largest and most profitable appliance manufacturer. Under the umbrella of Haier's now-powerful brand, Zhang began to diversify—first into air conditioners and freezers and later into washers and dryers, microwaves, televisions, and other consumer electronics.

The contracting manufacturing business expanded rapidly, taking Haier into the UK and Europe. It made further inroads through joint ventures with European and Japanese companies and by building manufacturing plants in Indonesia and Eastern Europe. Haier-built refrigerators sold particularly well in Germany, where their quality came to be recognized as not merely equal but superior to some well-regarded German brands. Not surprisingly, in 1997 Germany became the first export market for Haier-branded refrigerators—the opening shot in Zhang's global strategy to compete with the likes of Siemens, Electrolux, Whirlpool, Sony, Samsung, and GE. The same year, Haier formed a joint venture with the Philippine electronics company LKG to manufacture Haier-branded freezers, air conditioners, and washing machines in the Philippines for sale to local and regional markets. As it had in China, Haier differentiated itself by identifying customer-pleasing innovations and speeding them into production (for example, freezers with a separate compartment to keep ice cream soft, and—in Korea—a refrigerator compartment for pickling kimchi cabbage).

Soon the company widened its white-goods product range to include "black goods" (large consumer electronics such as televisions). Its "smart" appliances and televisions were among the items on display at the Consumer Electronics Show in Las Vegas in January 2012.

Haier tackled the U.S. market by sneaking under the radar of its big manufacturers, concentrating on niches where the company could quietly build its brand's reputation with retailers and consumers. One niche appeared in 1994 when Michael Jemal, a partner in the firm that imported Welbilt brand appliances, came looking for compact refrigerators suitable for offices and dormitories. He bought 150,000 of them to sell under the Welbilt name, and the whole batch sold within a year.

Haier quickly snatched up about a quarter of compact refrigerator sales, then branched into wine coolers and just as quickly won nearly a third of that market. In 2005, *Euromonitor* reported that Haier had U.S. market shares of 26 percent for compact refrigerators and 50 percent for wine coolers. All the time, Haier was adding new products, and Jemal was building relationships and the Haier brand with U.S. retailers. Walmart in particular became a big customer. In March 2005, Walmart's website listed forty-four different Haier products, most targeted to the college student market. The best-sellers were a $140 compact refrigerator, a 125-can beverage center for $165, and a $200 portable clothes washer. Topping Walmart's list of Haier products was a half-keg beer dispenser selling for $675.

Haier and Jemal formed a joint venture called Haier America, which planned to expand to a wider range of appliances where the established players had weaknesses. In 2000, it built a $40 million refrigerator factory in South Carolina. "We don't look to compete with them, because they are much bigger than we are," said Jemal. "We believe we have our separate position in the market and they have theirs. They can step on us anytime they want because we are so small compared to them in the U.S." To date, that philosophy seems to have prevailed, since Haier has yet to become a major player in larger appliances. In addition, the collapse of the housing market undoubtedly slowed its expansion strategy.

Most recently, Haier has set a goal of raising its market share in Europe, currently about one percent on major appliances. According to the *Financial Times*, "Haier's plan is to target the middle to upper end of the appliance market, rather than the low end traditionally associated with Chinese companies that compete mainly on price."[4] One thing that helps it, adds the FT, is that its name sounds more German than Chinese. "Most global consumers do not know it is Chinese. 'We never emphasize that point,' says Li Pan, managing director of Haier's overseas division. 'We don't deny it, but we don't emphasize it.'"

Between 2007 and 2010 Zhang undertook a major management innovation: scaling up a self-managing team technique normally confined to specific operations in plants and offices and turning it into a company-wide practice. Haier, he felt, needed to be extraordinarily responsive to its customers, able to move more swiftly than competitors in bringing innovations to market. To accomplish this, he organized the whole company into self-managing teams, ranging in size from ten or fewer members to roughly thirty, each focused on a retailing customer or group. The members include a minimum of four customer managers, four product managers, and a leader. The team members come from all levels and functions, but the ones who make the decisions are those who work directly with the customer. Each team within Haier is fully accountable for its decisions.

The result is a group that has both a close liaison with the customer and the ability to act instantly on what it learns from that customer. It is a powerful weapon against competitors anywhere. Because decision making is fast and accountability clear, the system ensures the fastest and most thorough possible integration of decisions. Essentially, it gives the global giant's customers the responsiveness they would expect from a local company.

Haier is still finding its way in the United States, and the great majority of its sales come from China. But its accumulated wins in markets almost everywhere give it unquestioned global status. With revenues of some $18 billion in 2011, it distributes products in more than 160 countries and regions. It has sixty-one trading companies, twenty-four manufacturing plants, ten R&D centers, and twenty-one industrial parks with more than seventy thousand people worldwide. In 2011, for the third year in a row, the Euromonitor International market research firm ranked it as the top appliance brand in the world, calculated its retail volume share as 7.8 percent, and named it a global leader in consumer electronics.

I'll leave the final word on Haier and Zhang to *Fortune* magazine's Geoffrey Colvin. Zeroing in particularly on Haier's system of self-managing teams, he writes: "Zhang is innovating radically, maybe more radically than any other manager operating on such a large scale. Even those who think they know him may not realize how far this former Red Guard and municipal bureaucrat is taking capitalism."[5]

THEY CAN CREATE INNOVATIVE NEW BUSINESS MODELS: BHARTI AIRTEL

If you still question whether leaders of the South have the ambition, tenacity, and business savvy to win in global markets, you should get to know Sunil Mittal. Until recent years few people outside of India had heard of Bharti Airtel, the telecom company he built from scratch. That changed abruptly when Mittal closed his transformative deal for the Zain Group's African assets in 2010. The $10.7 billion purchase of Zain, which included the Kuwait telecom company's African assets, was the largest-ever cross-border deal in the emerging markets, and it propelled Bharti Airtel into fifth place among global telecom companies. Fifty-five years old, Mittal had risen from modest beginnings to become one of the top business leaders in India, making headline news as CEO of the year, Indian businessman of the year, and one of the top entrepreneurs in the world. But Mittal did not consider his success to be the culmination of a dream. Rather, it was a stepping-stone in his long-term vision for the company to be counted among the best in the world.

Mittal's drive, tenacity, and business savvy are deeply rooted. Growing up in Ludhiana, a major industrial center in northern India, the young Mittal was surrounded by small metalworking and light-engineering shops where thousands of entrepreneurs made a living doing piecework and manufacturing components for larger industrial companies—goods like yarn to make hosiery and knitwear, and parts for motorcycles and bicycles. Ludhiana is the birthplace of Hero Honda, now the world's largest manufacturer of motorcycles by unit, and the hub of India's woolen knitwear industry, which when Mittal was coming of age in the late 1970s accounted for some 95 percent of India's knitwear exports.

Ludhiana was, in Mittal's words, "the bedrock of small-scale industry," and when he graduated from college at eighteen he immediately joined the game.[6] Borrowing $1,500 from his father, he set up a shop to forge crankshafts for bicycles, doing the grunt work of sales and distribution even if it meant riding in the backs of trucks and on crowded trains to stay within his meager budget. It was a viable way to eke out a living, but even at this young age Mittal saw the limitations of the business model: Bicycle manufacturers were many times larger than their suppliers and controlled the pricing and demand. Mittal didn't want such powerful players to put a ceiling on his ambitions, so after less than three years he moved to Mumbai, then called Bombay.

He started by buying diverse products—zippers, plastics, steel, and zinc—from foreign companies and reselling them to India's textile and metal industries. Then when he learned that Japan's Suzuki needed help selling portable generators in India, he convinced the company that he would be a reliable business partner and became its distributor. This was before the economic-liberalization policies of Prime Ministers Narasimha Rao and Manmohan Singh ignited India's economic growth and before India became the back office for Western multinationals. Until the late 1980s, government attempted to control India's economic growth through centralized planning and elaborate licensing requirements. An aspiring entrepreneur had to apply to enter a line of business, and there were often long delays and multiple approvals needed before permission was granted. The complex system, known as License Raj, was inefficient, susceptible to corruption, and protective of some businesses over others. Heavy tariffs and limits on foreign direct investment kept foreign competitors at bay, but that was small compensation for the unpredictable policies that could make or break a company or an industry overnight. In the early 1980s, the legislature suddenly banned generator imports, and as Mittal told an interviewer from *Knowledge@Wharton*: "One fine day, there was no business. All the business that I had developed was gone."[7]

What to do next? Mittal set out to trade fairs to find a product that would be unique, that he could afford, and, importantly, that wouldn't pit him against the big players back home. When he saw a push-button telephone at a show in Taiwan, he realized instantly that it would replace the rotary dial phones India had and that he could build a business around it. He persuaded Germany's Siemens AG to make him the Indian marketer and distributor of its phones and eventually expanded the business to include answering machines and fax machines.

Bigger opportunities took shape in the early 1990s as the Rao administration began to open up the economy. Better infrastructure was sorely needed, nowhere more so than in telecommunications, where India lagged far behind the United States, Europe, Japan, and Korea; millions of people in remote areas had no phone service at all. In 1992 the government announced that it was putting up for bid licenses that would allow private enterprise to compete with the three creaky government-controlled phone companies in a number of cities; Indian firms would be permitted to join with foreign ones in competing for the business. Mittal saw the beginning of a phenomenal growth curve. With just $5 million in sales, his company was out of contention for one of the $10 million licenses, so he put his skills to work enlisting partners. Ultimately he persuaded a French company (which later became

Vivendi) and telecom companies from Mauritius and the United Kingdom to partner with him.

His next challenge was to convince the government that his tiny company, then called Bharti Telecom, could be counted on to build a network and provide cell phone service as promised. Even his passion for the business and his foreign partners wouldn't be enough. He dedicated a full three months to mastering the details of his business plan and polishing his presentation to erase any doubts the decision makers might have. His efforts paid off: Bharti won one of two licenses for cell phone service in Delhi, India's second-largest city and, under the name Airtel, was the first of the eight new licensees to provide cell phone service in India. Mittal was where he wanted to be, at least for now: in on the ground floor of the telecom industry.

Financial success would not come easily. The initial investment was huge, the government put a cap on pricing, and competition soon arrived. The second license in Delhi was owned by Essar, a large, diverse twenty-five-year-old Indian company, and hand-to-hand combat broke out. But while Essar pursued large corporate clients, Airtel went broader, reaching out to small businesses and working fast to acquire the critical mass of customers needed to cover the investment in fixed assets. Despite the fast pace, Mittal ran a tight ship, because he knew operating discipline was essential to keeping costs low and customers happy. He protected the balance sheet by convincing handset suppliers to extend credit.

Bharti Airtel's focus on consumers proved to be the right choice, and the tiny upstart pulled ahead of Essar in Delhi. That gave Mittal all the encouragement he needed to pursue more licenses when the government put "circles"—essentially regions—up for bid. But this time hundreds of bidders were vying for the licenses, pushing prices sky high. Too high, according to Mittal's own calculations of what the licenses were worth. He came out with just two licenses, one to provide fixed-line phone service in central India and another to provide cell service in Himachal Pradesh in the north. He knew that introducing cell phones in Himachal Pradesh, a remote and sparsely populated mountainous area, would be very different from doing so in the Delhi market. But he also knew that success in those marginal markets would position him for business on a larger scale. Learning and winning on the periphery would prepare him to win in the most densely populated, most potentially profitable circles.

It wasn't long before new areas became available to him. By the late 1990s, some of the companies that had bid too high for cell phone licenses wanted to get out of their burdensome payments to the government and happily sold themselves at bargain prices. Mittal's company hadn't yet turned a profit, but he had established himself as a reliable and efficient operator. Financial partners, including SingTel and international private equity firm Warburg Pincus, signed on.

Mittal distanced his company from its many competitors with two crucial differentiators. The first was speed. Just as Mittal had beaten Essar in the Delhi market by getting the network up first and by broadening his reach, he rolled out new networks, new applications, and new approaches to pricing before others could move. "If you're caught between speed and perfection, always choose speed, and perfection will follow," Mittal said.[8] The second differentiator was staying close to customers. India is not one uniform consumer landscape. Consumer lifestyles, incomes, infrastructure, and state government initiatives or lack thereof are starkly different from state to state. For example, in Gujarat in the central west, the chief minister exercises extremely strong leadership in bringing in FDI and attracting industry from other states and has organizational machinery to execute swiftly under a democratic framework. He understands business, is driven to create economic growth, and has the social machinery to do so. In contrast, Bihar in the east was until three or four years ago ridden with crime in broad daylight. It is one of the richest states due to minerals and other natural resources, but it lacked law and order. It didn't attract industry; in fact, industry was leaving. A new chief minister got elected about eight years ago and is reinstating order. Industry is gradually coming in, but Bihar still has a long way to go. As Bharti entered these new markets, it relied on local managers, who were expected to understand the local conditions and be hands on in operationalizing the strategy.

The Indian government made one policy change after another, but Bharti Airtel adjusted. In 2003 the government lifted the restriction on the number of licenses a company could acquire, which unleashed an industry consolidation. From the necessity of competing against deep-pocketed operators such as Essar, Tata, and Reliance, which could afford to accumulate additional licenses, Mittal's business savvy led him to devise a new business model. The industry was not just growing but also changing fast. Yet revenue per subscriber was persistently low. So outcompeting others required reaching big numbers of consumers fast to achieve scale, while keeping those customers satisfied as their needs evolved from basic services to higher-value ones. The insight led to a unique business model that narrowed the managerial focus and freed up the capital for Mittal to pursue his ambitious vision. He outsourced the entire delivery system to other companies, farming out the information systems to IBM and the network building to Ericsson and Nokia Siemens (Siemens at the time). He paid them based on the traffic that came through the networks, effectively turning a business based on heavy fixed costs into one in which costs varied with usage. One of Airtel's great strengths had always been its sharp focus. This breakthrough model, which came to be known as the Indian model, further sharpened the focus. Now the company could pinpoint its efforts not just on telecom but specifically on telecom customers.

The Indian model is a radically new concept, totally different from the kind of outsourcing companies have done with their information technology. The most inventive part of this approach is that it reduces the capital intensity of the business by an order of magnitude, allowing the company to expand faster. Its supplier partners invest in and manage the infrastructure. They're business partners that have made a considerable financial investment and thus have skin in the game, and they share in the financial benefits of growth. If Airtel's revenues go up, the suppliers get paid more. If they go down, they get paid less. The exchange of information in real time and the day-to-day coordination of revenues, margins, and services are essential to maintaining trust in these long-term relationships.

Bharti Airtel's innovative business model allowed it to expand on a much bigger scale, perfect for an ambitious leader. As Mittal told the *Economic Times*: "Even in the year 2000, when Singapore's SingTel picked up a strategic stake in Airtel, we had just 3.5-lakh [350,000] customers. There were very few companies globally that had 25 million customers then. All the outsourcing deals that we did, be it IBM, Ericsson or Nokia Siemens, were to fulfill this one great dream of becoming a company with 25 million customers. But, once we got there, we set new targets, and for the first time we thought 100 million was possible. We achieved our target of 100 million one year ahead of what we had planned."[9]

In the early 2000s, Bharti Airtel continued to drive customer focus and operational excellence as it expanded geographically across India and then, for the first time, beyond India into Sri Lanka and Bangladesh. Whenever it entered new territory, it accumulated greater operational, managerial, and marketing scale while leveraging the business model that was the seed of its success: relying on partners to manage the information system and build the physical infrastructure and using local managers to focus hard on customers.

In making the deal for Zain, buying the telecom assets in fifteen African countries in one stroke, Mittal would use the same proven formula, taking partners IBM and Nokia Siemens into Africa with him. Manoj Kohli, an Indian professional who had led Bharti Airtel's South Asia business, would be chief executive of the company's international unit, but Africa would be largely run by Africans.

Industry watchers thought that the African cell phone industry was unmanageable and losing too much money and that Bharti Airtel had competition at home to worry about. But Mittal was banking on his proven efficiencies and customer focus. And he saw success in Africa as a huge step toward the ultimate goal of becoming number one or two in the world.

Bharti Airtel's ambitions for Africa were big: one hundred million subscribers and $5 billion a year in revenue in Africa by 2013 from forty-two million subscribers and annual revenue of $3.6 billion. Banks were not among the critics; in fact, they loved Bharti Airtel's business model and were eager to extend credit to what they saw as a telecom machine at the bottom of a steep growth curve. I cannot recall any instance in the last five decades (if ever) of a Sunil Mittal–type executive—a company's founder, major shareholder, and chairman—sending one of his top executives into a new territory to build a much smaller new acquisition. Kohli volunteered because the assignment will challenge and broaden him, and give him valuable global experience.

Kohli had led Bharti Airtel's operations in India, Bangladesh, and Sri Lanka and knew every detail of execution. He knew that what works in Gujarat doesn't necessarily work in Bihar, so his mind was open to figuring out the right approach for each of the fifteen African markets (today there are seventeen). He also understood the minds of Northern companies such as Vodafone, a major competitor in India. He had trained under Larry Bossidy, the legendary former CEO of Allied Signal and subsequently Honeywell, working in both those companies. Since he knew all the fundamentals, Kohli could improvise in each of the African markets, tweaking the specifics of the strategy (pricing, operations, reach to customers, working with individual governments, mix of service) to get it right. And Mittal had given him decision-making power.

Kohli didn't waste a moment in taking hold of the new acquisition, which meant learning the specifics of each country. "We tried to make it fast," he says. "In many cases the impact of integration is seen in two to three years. In our case it started within months, because we set the direction right from day one." It was an intensely hands-on process. "We consciously rejected consultants, for two reasons. One, all these guys have worked in Africa for ten or twenty years, and that's not the same as knowing the future. Second, we wanted to experience it for ourselves, with our own eyes and ears, make our own mistakes. Only then would we know the complexities and realities." He adds: "We would have to unlearn many things we knew, because past success does not guarantee future success."

Just a week after the acquisition was concluded, the company gathered the top one hundred African leaders in Kampala, the capital of Uganda, to jointly craft a vision for the future and answer questions. One of those questions, says Kohli, was "How long will you be here?" There was a lot of anxiety and cynicism, because the company had been acquired and divested five times over the previous ten or fifteen years. When the session ended, the vision made a clear statement about not only Airtel's direction but also its commitment: "Bharti will be the most loved brand in the daily lives of the African people by 2015."

Despite the difficulties of travel in Africa, where going to an adjacent country might mean routing through Paris or Dubai, Kohli went on the road for two months. He met with top government officials in each country, including the presidents, prime ministers, and various ministers and telecom regulators, and described to them in glowing terms how Bharti's services would contribute to Africa's economic development and better the lives of people. He visited Bharti's offices in each country, meeting as many employees as he could, shaking hands, and answering questions, so the local people could see "what sort of person" he was.

Bharti kept most of the original employees in place, apart from a few from Zain who went back to the Middle East. A few Indian leaders were brought in, but fewer than a hundred out of the 6,500 employees. About 85 percent of the top executives are African. Kohli sat with the top managers, tasking them to work on growth plans for the next three months and start on longer-term strategies. "You can't broad-brush strategies in Africa; you must customize to each market," he says. "There is nothing called Africa, like there's nothing called India. There are so many differences even within states. There are 10,000 languages, an average of four per country, and a thousand ethnic groups. You must bring a brand new mind-set to each." Nevertheless, all the country managers would have certain common tenets. Kohli ticks them off: "The basic ethics and values of the company, which we will not compromise. Our people culture: respect people, be sensitive cross-culturally. Be very aggressive in the market. Aim for affordable pricing, deep penetration into small towns and rural areas, and three specific growth paths: telephone, Internet, and money transfer—which is especially important because 95 percent of Africans had no access to banks." Finally he met with distributors and other stakeholders, along with the press, to whom he spelled out Bharti's investment plans (and tried to dispel some negative stereotypes about Indians—notably that they were stingy cost cutters).

A month later he returned for a second trip. "I went

back to reinforce what I'd said and make sure that they understood it," says Kohli. "Otherwise you're like the seagull that touches down and never goes back. We wanted to be sure they knew we would support them for much bigger success." All the time, the company was laying the groundwork for long-term relationships and building trust.

Bharti's African employees were initially disconcerted by the company's unique business model of splitting off various operations to partners. Some of them would now be working for IBM, Ericsson, or Huawei, and they didn't like it. It was explained that they would still be part of the Bharti Airtel family. To ease their anxieties, they were given letters stating that if they didn't like working for the other companies, they could come back to Airtel. "We worked with them case by case, partner by partner, and so far, nobody has wanted to come back to us," Kohli says.

The business model itself, the call centers, IT, distribution, and organizational design—all were "Africanized." For example, Bharti originally planned for three call centers, one for Francophone Africa, one for Nigeria, and one for the rest of Anglophone Africa. "That was wrong. We saw within months that it had to be changed because of the many different languages, lack of local connectivity, and regulatory issues. Today we have call centers in every country run by three partners. Gradually our suppliers picked up other customers such as banks and other telecom companies, so you could say we've given birth to a new service sector."

In what the company calls the second phase, starting around the end of 2011, it launched skill-building projects to upgrade the talent in each country. "Chad, for example, is in North Africa and half of it is desert. It's hard for people to get skills. We promised the government that we would build talent. And we're doing it, in IT, networking, finance, marketing—lots of training and orientation, sending people to India for a few weeks so they could see what we do there with their own eyes. They come back with fantastic motivation."

Headquarters in Delhi approves budgets, senior leadership appointments, and termination of any key appointment or long-term leader. Finance and HR staffs help to support the transformation, and operations are reviewed twice a quarter. "Otherwise," says Kohli, "the African team is empowered."

Kohli candidly acknowledges that getting Bharti's African venture sorted out has taken more time and money than the company had bargained for. "We haven't had net profit yet, a very important goal. Completing talent development will take another year or so. Our brand scores are improving, but they're not where we want them to be. We review each country, each project, each function, and pilot launches. The mechanism is very precise in terms of success factors. The transformation we initiated is significantly completed. The impact will come now, quarter by quarter."

Bharti is winning in four markets, the star being Kenya, and is poised to expand to the rest of the continent, with its additional five hundred million potential customers. In mid-2012 the company launched the fastest 3G technology in the world—HSPA plus—in all the markets, to become the largest 3G network in Africa, including in Nigeria.

The success in Africa makes Bharti truly global. By customer count it is, as of November 2012, the number four mobile phone operator, with more than 260 million customers. Its improving market cap will enable it to make more acquisitions and scale up.

My characterization of leaders and companies "of the South" is of course a generalization. Successes and failures occur everywhere for a variety of reasons. But my frequent visits to the South confirm my observation that Southern companies are on the move in ways many Northern companies still are not and might not even recognize. They are using inventive strategies and business models combined with fundamental business skills. Could companies of the South be derailed? Yes, of course they could: If their eyes are bigger than their stomachs. If their ambition is too grandiose and falls out of step with their internal re-sources. If they become impervious to early warning sig-nals that someone else is changing the game. Or if they get too comfortable and let execution slide.

The point for other companies is not to wait for those derailments but to see that despite the structural changes that the long-term unstoppable trends in technology, government, demographics, and digitization are caus-ing, some leaders are finding a path. They're imagining a very different competitive landscape ten to twenty years out and figuring out how they can participate in it. They consider what areas are most attractive according to their growth potential and what it will take to win in them. They think big, and with each new success they build con-fidence to pursue the next great opportunity.

You live in the same world. Do you have the same confidence, the same ability to imagine a future in which your company succeeds? Are you willing to work hard at it? The following chapters explain why you might need to think differently about strategy, why your leadership may have to change, and how you might have to change your organization to make it fit for the tilt. The final chapter of the book describes three Northern companies that are suc-ceeding, proving that any company with the right combi-nation of strategy, leadership, organization, and execution can win in the tilt.

PART II

HOW TO SUCCEED
IN THE GLOBAL TILT

CHAPTER FOUR

OUTSIDE IN & FUTURE BACK

STRATEGY FOR A TILTED WORLD

Think about some large numbers:

One billion new consumers added to the world economy in the past decade.

Two billion more joining in the coming decade.

$2 trillion (give or take a few billion) of new economic growth annually in the coming decade.

After struggling through the arid lands of parched growth for years, you stand on a dune overlooking this immense lake of opportunity. Now, are you going to approach it with a teaspoon or a bucket?

It's not a trick question. Many businesspeople of the

North have become conditioned to think small, because they've been fighting for incremental gains in scrubby markets. Unless they break the habit, they will bring teaspoons. Only bold and ambitious thinkers will come with buckets.

In the 1980s, 1990s, and early 2000s, though the business environment grew steadily more turbulent, mainstream companies could still survive through gradual change, honing core capabilities and creatively extending them to new markets. But pursuing incremental change in the context of the global tilt is not a reliable path to success. Human imagination and drive and the transparency of interconnectedness across the globe will help global GDP to grow 3 percent–plus a year for the next decade, even taking into account ongoing setbacks caused by the financial meltdown. At the end of ten years the total world economy will be on the order of $85 trillion.

Get yourself a bucket—and be prepared to change the way you do business. Increasingly, the life of a strategy is getting shorter and new and creative business models are emerging, sending the old ones to the trash heap. No matter what your model, at some point it will become irrelevant or obsolete or will lose value against new competitors and new opportunities. That point can arrive abruptly, without clear advance signals. Consider, for example, the reversed fortunes of Research In Motion (RIM) and

Nokia, two of the leading power players in mobile phones up to 2006. As of this writing—scarcely six years after their dominance seemed assured—both are in deep trouble, beaten down by competitors with newer ideas, better technology, and closer contact with the marketplace. Heroic efforts to revive them may have come too late.

Staying ahead of the game will more and more require fresh thinking, attention to innovation—your own and others'—and expanding your horizons.

IT'S TIME TO UNLEARN OLD LESSONS

The central mental skill of leadership today is the ability to identify long-term, large-scale opportunities and then build the capabilities to turn them into reality. The problem for many leaders is that this new turn in the road leads directly away from lessons they've learned for much of their careers: Stick to your knitting; stay with your core competencies. And as we shall see, the lesson has also been drilled into the minds of investors, who as a result take a dim view of bold ventures that might compromise near-term financial performance.

The concept of core competencies, introduced by C. K. Prahalad and Gary Hamel in 1990 to describe an organization's unique strengths, has helped many leaders focus their business. In particular it has helped solve the problem of investing resources in non-value-adding activities or those the company was not especially good at. The outsourcing trend of the 1990s was largely driven by this kind of thinking, whereby businesses shed activities others could do better. Along the same line, Bain & Company partner Chris Zook has documented the importance of preserving and leveraging the company's core business. Zook's research catalogues the many failures that result when leaders lose sight of their core and argues persuasively that companies can unlock growth potential by extending and building on core strengths that are underutilized.

The concepts developed by Prahalad and Hamel and Zook are widely used in designing and developing corporate and business unit strategies; they are reliable guides to incremental growth, but there is a flaw. They make leaders internally focused and biased toward leveraging existing capabilities. This internal orientation puts you at risk of missing serious threats to the core business, some of which might require new capabilities. The way I see it, strategy making as usual is basically an inside-out, rearview-mirror approach that too often misses the opportunity or necessity for large-scale change.

Kodak provides a classic example. In the late 1990s it expanded its film business into China, an untapped market that then-CEO George Fisher found enticing. It was virtually impossible to get nationwide access to China back then, and Fisher worked tirelessly to develop relationships with Chinese state-owned enterprises, provincial governments, city governments, ministries, commissions, and banks, and spoke of having Zhu Rongji, who became Chinese prime minster in 1998, as a tennis partner. Eventually the doors opened. In 1998 the company committed to invest $1.2 billion in two joint ventures to manufacture and distribute film, paper, and photochemical products in the country. Fisher wisely established the ventures in a way that gave local partners minority stakes in exchange for business assets, ensuring that Kodak would have operational control. Despite the political risk, it seemed that Kodak was making a breakthrough, and investors approved.

But while the Chinese deals expanded Kodak's core business, they did nothing to solve its bigger problem: the shift to digital photography. Kodak had been pioneering digital technology since the 1970s. It had a crude prototype of a digital camera as early as 1975 and in the mid-1990s helped Apple develop its QuickTake 100 digital camera. Competing in digital technology was, however, a different game altogether and one that threatened Kodak's core business. For one thing, the company didn't dominate the field the way it did in film but was one of many players—599 by one count.[1] The market was also less predictable, and margins were lower. Much lower. According to a former executive, gross margins on the traditional business were a whopping 75 percent.

Securities analysts liked the business as it was: highly profitable. Only in hindsight did they see the need for Kodak to move faster into digital. Longtime Kodak employees also liked the status quo and were resentful of the digital team.[2] So while Fisher recognized the growing importance of digital imaging, the realities of organizational resistance and Wall Street myopia seem to have kept him from making a different, more radical strategic bet, and the old business commanded the resources and management attention for too long. Later efforts to speed the transition to digital were unable to stem Kodak's decline, and in January 2012 this great innovation company with a pioneering legacy—a brand once revered around the world and holding more than a thousand digital-imaging patents—filed for bankruptcy.

Expect to see a lot of unhappy stories (not necessarily as poignant) as the tilt makes more competencies obsolete or less relevant. But astute leaders who have the discipline and courage to shed a core competency that is becoming obsolete or marginal can make the transition successfully and even profitably. GE's top management foresaw that the move into plastics by the Saudi Arabian public-private partnership SABIC would ultimately alter the competitive game. Plastics was a profitable core GE business, whose distinguished alumni include former CEO Jack Welch, current CEO Jeff Immelt, and former vice chairmen John Krenicki and John Opie. But neither profits nor sentiment kept these men from looking at the business with clear eyes. They realized that one of the unit's core competencies was no longer going to be differentiated, given the incoming competition and commoditization. Reshuffling their portfolio for the future global game, they sold the plastics division to SABIC for roughly $11 billion.

The tilt creates an imperative for all leaders, from frontline managers to the CEO, to look at the business from the *outside in,* that is, through the lens of a leader sitting elsewhere and looking at the global changes uncontaminated by your underlying assumptions and rules of thumb. You have to take a fresh look at the world, and in a sense, look out of the corner of your eye to see how forces that seem unrelated to your business could interact and combine to create opportunities and threats to your industry or company. No matter what your business model, at some point it will become irrelevant or obsolete against new competitors and new opportunities. At that point the value of the business may drop sharply. If you're vigilant in looking from the outside in, you'll see when that time is coming—soon or many years away—in time for you to make a move. You'll know when radical steps such as cutting a product line, selling a division, or reinventing the business model are needed to prevent the decline.

"Outside in" will help you detect not only threats but also opportunities. They're often not obvious from the macro trends and may require some second-order thinking to be discovered. For example, we know China targets certain industries it wants to dominate; you will almost surely want to avoid tackling them head-on. But can you hitch a ride? What resources—raw materials, energy, or talent—will those industries require and how will China get them? If technology is needed, will China allow more foreign companies in? What opportunities does that create for a company in the North?

This scenario is playing out right now in China's automotive industry, which sells about eighteen million vehicles a year. The goal is to ramp production up to thirty-six million a year twenty years out. China badly needs auto parts to reach its goal, and it's allowing parts suppliers to invest there without the usual tough demands for technology transfer. That's a huge growth opportunity for suppliers, one they could miss by looking from the inside out. But Delphi looked from the outside in and spotted the opportunity early. Today it has sixteen wholly owned and joint-venture plants where it is the majority partner (and thus in control) and two research and development centers in China. It plans to expand production capacity in those plants and is also considering several new factories to meet growing demand.

Just as important as outside in is *future back*. By this I mean you must extend your time horizon as you assess the world and imagine what the competitive landscape will be some twenty years out. Then jump back to consider its implications for the present. For example, it's likely that in twenty years there will be more cars in China than in the United States, and the segmentation of the market will have changed. Many of those vehicles will be in urban centers—as many as twenty million cars in one city, by some estimates. Would that create the impetus for battery-powered cars? Where will the key ingredients for those batteries come from? From that picture of the future, think about the size and characteristics of the markets. Where would you want to be? Then work backward to what you must do now to get there. In particular, think about the capabilities you'll have to build to take you from where you are to where you'd like to be. And at the same time, consider what great capabilities your company has that won't really count much in the future—for example, design expertise in materials that are no longer cutting edge. In short, future back is the exact opposite of focusing on the core capabilities you have now and seeking ways to extend them into new areas—usually adjacent markets, such as a brand that can be used in another segment of the company's current customer base.

You cannot define your path in the tilt without thinking outside in and future back. I'm not suggesting that a company should abandon its core, but a wider lens can help you see that your company may need to change sooner and on a bigger scale. Your failure to build the necessary new capabilities and remove the ones that are obsolete will take you to oblivion given today's speed of change. Do you have the courage to acknowledge when existing strengths and incremental change are not enough—when what's required is a new direction, a major shift in emphasis, or a capability your company lacks? Are you willing to shed old capabilities to make room for new ones? To succeed in the tilt, you must not only think more broadly but also move more decisively. You must be prepared to make an occasional big move.

GET READY FOR STRATEGIC BETS

Strategic bets are big, bold moves that have the potential to shake up the company, the industry, and sometimes other industries. Their purpose is to put the company on a new growth trajectory or take it off a downward path—

or both. They are game changers that entail considerable risk, and because their outcome is uncertain, they almost always stir up angst and meet resistance, most often from Wall Street. In fact, you know you're making a strategic bet when you feel the stress that comes from staring risk in the face. Succeeding in a tilted world requires that you know when it's the right time to make such a bet, for offensive or defensive reasons. This is where an outside-in, future-back view is an invaluable survival tool. You'll need toughness to make the bet, and also to withstand the challenges and pushback you'll inevitably get when you make one.

That's what Andrew Liveris, the CEO of Dow Chemical, demonstrated when he bet the future of his business on the acquisition of Rohm and Haas in July 2008. Liveris saw changes brewing in the chemicals industry. Looking outside in and future back, he realized that sooner or later the playing field would tilt away from Dow's long-held strengths. For decades it had been the dominant player in the commodities chemical business, processing crude oil into a range of petrochemicals sold to a multitude of industries. But new players from Asia and the Middle East were coming into the industry. At the same time, oil producers were getting interested in businesses that processed their raw materials. Liveris imagined how a direct competitor like SABIC, whose majority shareholder is the Saudi Arabian government, might combine with a Saudi Arabian oil producer's drive for vertical integration. He concluded that advantages in access to and pricing of crude would make it all but impossible for Dow to retain its number one position in the low-margin commodities business. Because of its pricing disadvantage, Dow couldn't win in the new game, and at some point the company's market value would decline.

Liveris saw a brighter future for Dow in higher-margin specialty products. To win in that area, it would have to strengthen its limited capability. This would be the very essence of a big bet, requiring Dow to radically shrink its mainstay business in favor of something that was only a minor part of its business. And the bet had to be made quickly, ahead of the competition and before Dow's market value took a nosedive.

The Rohm and Haas acquisition would shore up Dow's capabilities in specialty chemicals, but at $18.8 billion the all-cash deal required more than Dow had. Now Liveris had to really stick his neck out, tapping out Dow's resources and patching together financing. To fill the gap, he signed an agreement for a joint venture with Kuwait's state-run Petrochemical Industries Company (PIC), which would infuse Dow with $9 billion to partly finance the deal. It was the first joint venture between the two parties, and Liveris's plan to acquire Rohm and Haas hinged on its success.

Liveris had the stomach to make the strategic bet, which rested precariously on the deal with PIC. His frequent communication with the board of directors and institutional investors brought them along with him. He paved the way by putting together a meticulous plan and meeting frequently with the board to discuss financing the deal, what to divest, and whether the timing was right. Wall Street didn't like the deal when it was announced in July 2008. Analysts thought the change in direction was too sudden, the acquisition too expensive, and the outcome too uncertain, even given Dow's solid balance sheet and standing as the industry leader in sales. Yet Liveris and the board did not back down, because they understood what would happen to Dow if it did not make the bet. They bet that it would be only a matter of time before analysts and rating agencies caught up with them. They had the confidence and stamina to persevere even when the global financial crisis erupted that fall.

Then on December 31, 2008, two days before the joint venture with PIC was to close, the high stakes of Dow's strategic bet became visceral: The Kuwaiti government abruptly backed out, throwing Liveris's plan into jeopardy. Most observers expected Dow Chemical to retreat, but doing so would have put the company in a tough legal situation. The contract with Rohm and Haas was airtight and its leaders wouldn't budge. In the wake of the financial crisis, finding a replacement for PIC's promised investment wouldn't be easy. Even in normal times, investors are often fearful about committing money to a strategic bet, but at that moment, as the capital markets were coping with the worst economic crisis in sixty-five years and the world financial system was teetering, their fear was compounded. Both the debt markets and the equity firms were paralyzed, and the stock market was in free fall. Dow's own stock, which had been at thirty dollars a share when the deal was announced, plummeted to seven dollars by March 2009. Dow faced the prospect of a debt downgrade to junk status by Standard & Poor's and Moody's.

Shocked by PIC's move, Liveris nonetheless had to keep the board committed to the deal, find new sources of financing, and convince the capital markets that Dow's strategy had hit a bump, not a brick wall. In the end, he succeeded. He kept the directors on board, convinced the ratings agencies to maintain the company's investment-grade rating, and lined up financing from Warren Buffett and two members of the Rohm and Haas family. And the deal was in fact transformational; it set up a combined Dow–Rohm and Haas enterprise for better performance than either company might have expected alone and put the company on a growth track rather than a downward slide. Today specialty chemicals make up about two-thirds of Dow's revenue, up from 50 percent before the merger, and Liveris says he is aiming to tilt the mix toward 80 percent.

If Liveris hadn't been thinking outside in and future back, if he hadn't had the courage to acknowledge that control of crude oil by foreign governments would favor Dow's competitors, he would not have seen the need to make a sudden move, especially when he did. He positioned the company for the new game that was just beginning to take shape, not the old game Dow had already played. And while Dow's move caused others in the industry to reconsider their positioning and competitive edge, it was far enough ahead that it didn't have to fight its way through a bidding war.

Earnings have become less volatile since then: Dow was able to raise prices 5 percent in 2011, which more than offset increases in purchased feedstock and energy costs. Its stock price—please pay attention, short-termers—has more than rebounded from the low of $5.75 in 2009 to $33 in April 2012. In his analysis of the company in February 2012, Standard & Poor's equity analyst Leo J. Larkin wrote: "We think long-term results for Dow will benefit from the company's strategy of shifting the business portfolio to less cyclical specialty chemicals and plastics as well as the expansion into agricultural products. . . . Following its merger with Rohm and Haas in 2009, the company has been gradually reducing the balance sheet leverage. We believe this will help position the company to grow via internal investment and joint venture investments."

There are two basic reasons that every leader must be prepared to make a strategic bet in the coming years, maybe even more than once in a decade.

First, to put a stake in the ground. Companies mark off the territory to gain a future advantage—by creating a new business or new capability, for example, or by winning control over an input that will be critical to success. Markets, capabilities, and resources are already being hotly contested. For example, some leaders make a strategic bet to secure a raw material they need to ensure they can pursue market segments they've targeted. That's why Toyota acquired a large portion of a lithium mine and production facility in Argentina in January 2010. The aim was to secure access to the rare element used in lithium-ion batteries, a key technology in hybrid cars. In the early 2000s, Verizon, under the leadership of CEO Ivan Seidenberg, made a $22 billion bet when the company put fiber-optic cable in the ground against the advice of just about everybody, including shareholders. But that gutsy decision has paid off well.

Second, to shed tired assets and move on. When the business model or a major asset becomes obsolete, its market value sharply declines. The business might still be making money, but if the industry is moving toward commoditization, for example, pricing power will begin to slip. Eventually, as the financials suffer and investors take notice, the market value of the business drops. It's a strategic bet to pull out ahead of that decline and shift resources and energy into something with more promise. One of your jobs as a leader is to pragmatically and unflinchingly evaluate the value of your assets and the robustness of your business model on a long-term basis and move before their value deteriorates.

In 1996, Allied Signal CEO Larry Bossidy made exactly that sort of move. He had transformed the company after taking over in 1991 by paying close attention to execution and leadership development. He was particularly proud of raising the profitability of the auto parts business, which accounted for 15 percent of sales. But judging that automakers were facing a significant revenue decline in the years ahead, he sold most of it in order to focus on the more attractive aerospace and chemical products. Three years later, Allied Signal was well positioned for its merger with Honeywell.

No strategy has an infinite life. You should rigorously watch ahead of time for signs that conditions are likely to change. When will value—not just earnings—begin to decline? What will cause or accelerate that decline—

currency, competition, technology, consolidation, customers' changing lifestyles? Remember that change can
be your friend, and go on the offensive.

The Thomson Corporation, now Thomson Reuters,
was a profitable publisher of regional newspapers and professional journals in Canada and the United States in the
late 1990s. But CEO Dick Harrington saw clouds gathering beyond the industry's horizon. Big national retailers
like the Gap and Target were launching national media
campaigns and putting a squeeze on regional department
stores, which had to cut back on advertising. When the
big chains advertised in newspapers, they used circulars,
which were less profitable than the traditional display ads
department stores had been placing in Thomson's newspapers. At the same time, the Internet browser was catch-
ing on, and Harrington recognized it as a threat to the
classified ads that accounted for half of Thomson's bottom
line.

Had he been wedded to the concept of core competence, Harrington would have fought to protect the newspapers, tweaking the business model, as many publishers
have done since. Instead, seeing that the current trends
were irreversible and would eventually make it impossible
to create value, he made a strategic bet to exit newspapers
altogether and expand Thomson's information services.
He saw that professional publishing was a growth area

and, using Thomson's existing specialty and professional publications as a base, set out to build a business around the electronic provision of specialized information: legal and regulatory, financial services, scientific research, health care, and education. In the next several years, the company spent some $7 billion to acquire more than two hundred businesses it had painstakingly researched for their strategic fit and financial viability. In other words, Thomson shed the business it knew best when it was at the top of its game for the sake of increasing its chances of success in the future. Thomson had a market value of around $8 billion at the time. Today, Thomson Reuters is worth some $23 billion.

It's worth noting that making a strategic bet is not synonymous with merger and acquisition activity, although M&A may be a vehicle for a strategic bet. Many companies sell a division to gain some cash or because it's more valuable to the acquirer, but unless it alters the fate of the company, it's not a strategic bet.

For those who think strategic bets are too risky, consider the risk of *not* making one: it can marginalize the business, meaning its value will decline and its fate may fall into the hands of a hostile acquirer, a competitor, or the government.

Even companies that see growth within easy reach have to look at the business from the outside in and future back. Companies in the South, for instance, have rich opportunities in their own backyard and clear advantages over foreigners, who often have trouble understanding the local conditions. But they too need to look beyond their immediate surroundings and further out, then move at least as fast as the speed of the game. If they don't get the essential building blocks in place now—important capabilities, market presence, or access to resources—other companies could well build scale ahead of them and outcompete them in their home markets.

FIGHT THE SHORT-TERM BEAST

The highest duty of a business leader should be to build long-term economic value. But publicly held companies in the North face a conundrum: How do you think ten or twenty years out when Wall Street thinks short term? Total shareholder return (TSR) is a key measure for companies traded on the New York Stock Exchange. One problem with TSR is that it doesn't always reflect the real economic return of a company, since it's also a function of the bets placed by players in the capital markets. This means that executive compensation linked to TSR does not necessarily reflect how well leaders have actually *run* the business. Nonetheless, it has created a kind of tyranny in decision making that tips the short-term/long-term balance heavily toward the next four quarters. Favoring the short term can permanently handicap a company and its entire ecosystem for the long run. It takes skill and courage to resist the pressure when the owners of capital are represented vociferously by middlemen such as fund managers, whose compensation rests on delivering near-term profits. (It's yet one more dysfunctional aspect of the global financial system: The self-interest of the financial-services industry can work against the future prosperity of the company, its true owners, and the nation.)

The practical realities of institutional investing reinforce the short-term focus: Many intermediaries that have big funds to invest lack the manpower and time to evaluate the fundamentals of every publicly traded company. They rely on ratings by third parties, such as Institutional Shareholder Services, which ranks a company's governance based in part on whether the board of directors uses TSR as a basis for CEO compensation.

With as much as 80 percent of their annual compensation at stake, business leaders vigilantly protect margins, even if it means passing up markets that would put them on a path to faster growth. Meanwhile, competitors put their stakes in those market spaces, which are open now but might be hard to enter later. Many Southern companies, especially those backed by their governments, drive for market share and scale, for which they'll willingly accept lower price points, lower absolute margins, and in many cases lower percentage margins. They figure that whatever is not strong now—whether it's sales, profit margins, the supply chain, or product quality—will gradually improve. Think about the telecom space in Africa, where Bharti Airtel is prepared to withstand the short-term lack of profit as it builds the customer base and increases usage per customer. Success there will allow it to build another base in another geography and lead in the chess game of global market share. Will AT&T, Sprint, Verizon, and telecom in Europe have a rude awakening later when Bharti has amassed customers across several continents and is sniffing out its next frontier? (Britain's Vodafone is wide awake and looking outside in; it's competed against Bharti in India for years and is competing against it in Africa.)

You have to accept that the context is different in other parts of the world. For global products, such as Apple's, you have to wrestle with how to increase brand awareness and build global share at rock-bottom prices and margins because of differences in purchasing power, and you have to do so without cannibalizing the business in higher-price regions. In other cases, lower purchasing power demands an entirely different customer experience. Thinking outside in, you might see the need to redesign the product, the business model, or the whole value chain. While it may be necessary to accept smaller margins in critical markets, you can control other variables that affect your return on invested capital. You could, for instance, scale up faster or increase the asset turnover and thereby boost the rate of profitable growth. Remember too that you may end up trimming margins and making these moves at some later point, when your inaction has put you on the defensive.

TSR can also force companies to pass up acquisitions that would strengthen their competitive position. Consolidation and cost cutting are considered legitimate rationales for mergers and acquisitions in the North, but winning in a broader, longer-term game is not, the expansive rhetoric of many merger announcements notwithstanding. Businesses shy away from deals that are strategically uncertain and that don't promise to boost earnings anytime soon. Yet those targets may be utterly necessary in the long term.

It may appear impossible to compete against companies with twenty-year time horizons. But it is unwise if not downright irresponsible for leaders to compromise the company's future. Rather than surrender to short-termism, leaders need to take a stand and sharpen their thinking about Wall Street's demands.

Clearly communicate the logic of your short-term/long-term balance and direction—to investors if you're a CEO, to your higher-ups if you're a middle manager. If you are in fact building a marathon company, say so—

explicitly and frequently. The real issue for managers is building credibility in their efforts to balance the short term and the long term through execution. Wall Street hits companies hardest when they fail to deliver what they promise, especially if the reasons for missing were under management's control. But if you execute well and consistently deliver (and not by borrowing from the following year), investors will tend to hold the stock longer term. CEOs and their chief financial officers can cultivate a shareholder base that thinks this way. It sometimes happens that an industry is out of favor or a company's stock is oversold, opening a gap between its market price and its intrinsic value and making the company an attractive acquisition target. Even in those unusual situations, leaders should damn the torpedoes and build credibility through disciplined execution against realistic goals.

Investing in the future is built into the budgets at IBM, Johnson & Johnson, Amazon.com, and many other publicly traded companies. The market supports their versions of short-term/long-term balance. And it catches up with companies that invest too little in their futures. HP, for example, is coming under pressure for having spent too little on R&D in recent years; CEO Meg Whitman is now increasing R&D spending and candidly acknowledges that it will be a long haul to recover HP's market value. In September 2012 Procter & Gamble came under fire for its lack of breakthrough products, perhaps the result of division managers being put in charge of innovation yet held responsible for short-term operating results.

Others still may remain unpersuaded, but you have to have conviction, communicate, and establish some goalposts against which to measure your progress. TSR imposes one kind of discipline. But leaders need to use their own judgment. Know where the business needs to be and what must be done to get there—and deliver both the message and the results with discipline.

CHANGE YOUR PSYCHOLOGY

Outside-in, future-back thinking is one way to break mental barriers, but other kinds of psychological blockages can prevent you from seeing a clear path forward. Every one of us has a lens, or frame of reference, deeply etched in us by experience and education, through which we see the world. Each of us has subconscious guidelines that govern our behaviors and decision making. We all make assumptions that may never be challenged. Success reinforces them and etches them more deeply. Business leaders who have climbed the ranks by improving margins through cost cutting or premium pricing, for instance, tend to look for that skill in the people they hire and promote, because to them, it's what leadership success is made of. They themselves have been rewarded for such thinking throughout their careers.

You can't let an outdated frame of reference stop you from seeing reality. It's easy for leaders in the North to be complacent if they believe that the South will take a long time to catch up. That's wishful thinking. Already some Southern companies have revenues high enough to be in the Fortune 50. In most industries, it won't be more than five or ten years before more Southern companies' products and services will be good enough to challenge even the strongest companies in the North—and on their home turf. China is poised to win in automobiles and aircraft and has its sights set on pharmaceuticals. Brazil is strong in regional jets. India dominates in back-office automation and business processing and will continue to move into higher-value products and services, such as data analysis, partly through companies such as Accenture, IBM, and Microsoft that have located there.

India has the momentum to win in some segments of pharmaceuticals five or ten years out and is already competitive in generics. As the number of patents filed by large pharmaceutical companies has fallen, some have acquired Indian companies for their manufacturing capability and market presence.

Remember: We're talking here not about labor and currency arbitrage but about the growing number of businesses that outcompete the North with managerial prowess and technological sophistication. They have highly trained, entrepreneurial leaders who use outside experts to help them build fundamental business capabilities and processes. Huawei Technologies, for example, the Chinese telecommunications equipment maker that overtook Alcatel-Lucent and Nokia Siemens to become number two in the world, has hired a number of experienced executives from the North, including a Swede to head its wireless marketing unit and a German to head its handset design, and retains consultants from IBM and KPMG. In 2010 *Fast Company* rated Huawei the fifth most innovative company in the world.

The leadership skill behind companies in the South is a force to be reckoned with. People in the North who have never spent time in the South and get their information secondhand can easily underestimate the players and misgauge where the battlefield is going to be. Passed-on information might not capture the entrepreneurial drive and fast decision making that are common or the psychological and emotional energy of the leaders there. It can miss the pragmatism that makes some leaders willing to take on joint-venture partners with limited control for the sake of shoring up competencies they lack.

The best leaders in the South are not only as hard driving and talented as the best in the North: Their psychology is different in crucial ways. Because of the circumstances under which they've lived, been educated, and built their careers, their mind-set is to accept as givens the scarcity of resources for themselves and their customers. As he built the $16 billion metals business under the Birla aegis, Debu Bhattacharya, managing director of Hindalco, had to focus on the fundamentals while dealing with the vagaries of the government and with limited resources. Now in his sixties, he continues to work seven days a week overseeing management, acquisitions, operations, and innovation. An engineer by training and a former plant manager, he understands the nuts and bolts of the business. Yet he sees the bigger picture and has the business acumen to cut through the issues incisively. Risk is a given for many of these leaders. So are the idiosyncrasies of legislative and regulatory actions, which they've learned to tolerate. Like Bhattacharya, many business leaders have come up through engineering schools and are adept with numbers and drilling into operational details. The best of them are also great judges of people, which means they're good at finding talent to take them where they want to go, and they'll cut their losses quickly if the person doesn't work out.

When one of India's big industrial companies ventured into a road-construction project, the CEO was clear and precise about what phase one would require: the ability to pull together four different state governments, the federal government, and three to four financial backers—not an inconsequential task in India. He chose a person who had shown that he had the temperament and experience to put such deals together. Execution was not this person's strength, nor did it have to be, at least for the first six months. After that the CEO would move him to another assignment where he could shine, replacing him with a person skilled at execution. The sharp definition of the job and the person's talent were what mattered and what made the difference for the company.

Leaders in the North may be unsure of how to expand in the South. Perhaps they don't know how to develop and manage people in vastly different cultures or are afraid to commit resources to areas they know little about and whose political and regulatory environments are so unpredictable. Maybe they just don't have the stomach to deal with foreign governments and local conditions. They might be put off by reports of corruption in India, China, and Africa and justify caution on that basis.

Those blockages can cause them to miss the other side of that equation: the learning they're missing out on by not being there, facing the skirmishes, building the networks of information and goodwill. By postponing the learning, they give competitors an edge. GE, 3M, and Yum! Brands' KFC chain all put people on the ground early to learn the local culture and business environment. Living there is different from reading about a country or flying in for three-day visits. As CEO of Nalco, the Illinois-based water services and treatment company, Erik Fyrwald spent weeks at a time in India over several years to learn the nuances of the country. It's what gave him confidence to successfully expand the business there.

Even industries the Chinese government targets, such as wind power, leave room for competitors who have the managerial capacity and will to compete, because those spaces are so big. Industries that are not on the government's radar leave more elbow room. KFC earns higher margins in China than in the United States. Companies like John Deere and Caterpillar have been in China for decades and are flourishing there. Makers of luxury goods from the United States, the UK, and Europe are opening stores in many urban centers and drawing the South's newly affluent customers.

Now the horizon is clear and your choices are overwhelming. It's like taking flight when you've been driving a car. Suddenly you have three dimensions to navigate instead of two, and the options seem infinite. Which direction will you fly? There are many right answers. Shape mutually exclusive options for the future of your company without the constraints of existing capabilities or core competencies. That's what outside in, future back is all about.

Choose a central idea you want to pursue or a direction you want to move in, then work out the details and specifics to develop a full-fledged strategy that is unique to your company. Be sure you know what capabilities you need to build, and what risks you're taking and how you'll manage them. Remember, it is ultimately leaders, not businesses, that compete. You'll need clear thinking and a willingness to stick your neck out to find the right path and the right pace. Clarity of thought and the perspiration needed to achieve your ambition are worth a thousand IQ points. Then the universal business rule applies: You have to execute. No execution, no results.

Execution here means mobilizing your organization to the reality of the global tilt. It's about equipping people for transition: changing their mind-sets, getting them to align with the new state you want to be in, and understanding the social tools you will need to do these things.

In the next two chapters I will detail the requisite leadership capabilities and organizational changes. I will start with a capability that has the jaw-breaking name of "multicontextual." Does that sound like jargon? When you get to the meaning behind it, you'll see that it's very real—and a big deal.

CHAPTER FIVE

MASTERING MULTIPLE CONTEXTS

LEADERSHIP IN A TILTED WORLD

S ome things about leadership never change. Leaders decide what an organization does and doesn't do. They figure out ways to create value and spot new opportunities. They find new ways of managing. They select and grow leaders who will build the future, and so forth. The tilt has raised the bar with something new and different. Now you are going to have to be "multicontextual," a word that only recently moved out of academia and into the mainstream. Here I refer to the strategic and cultural contexts that frame your business activities in different regions and countries. These contexts include all the variables unique to each country, everything from how the government operates and who's who in the informal social networks to how distribution systems work and what gives local competitors an edge. Learning the local language, being empathetic, and respecting local mores only scratch the surface of what you must do. You will need to master multiple local contexts quickly and accurately, distilling the key factors and new rules of thumb for each place.

Your insights about the local context are crucial inputs to judgments on business issues. Selecting and assigning people, deciding what markets to enter in what sequence at what pace, allocation of resources—these and other crucial decisions rest on accurate depiction of the most important factors in each geography. If you're not multi-contextual, you're likely to miss specific local needs and opportunities—and the trade-offs you make or advocate will be misinformed.

Leadership that is not multicontextual is a common problem for Northern companies. Almost all businesses are organized around functions (such as finance or human resources), headquarters, and geographies. Some also have reporting hierarchies for business units or product lines. Tension arises among these organizational silos as each tries to influence priorities and resource allocation. Making trade-offs between headquarters, business units, product lines, and business functions is familiar ground that leaders generally traverse well. But information from geographic units is often subject to mental filters. Unless the leader is multicontextual, perceptions and even facts become distorted. It doesn't help that smaller geographies often report through regional leaders, who rarely are truly multicontextual.

Global leadership means discerning the fundamentals in each context and bringing them into the broader context of the company as a whole, and then mobilizing people to accomplish the business goals. Almost every country has a local vocabulary for the concepts used to measure and run a business—things like cash, margins, capital invested, and debt. In India, for example, even large industrialists tend to speak in Urdu, the language used by street vendors. Cash is *nakad*, capital is *zama*, debt is *kurtz*, and profit is *nafa*. (The inflections, too, are often those of the street vendor: if the *nafa* is less than desired, the tone may be faintly dismissive, and accompanied by an outward rolling of the hand.) But whatever the language, the underlying concepts are universal.

Global leaders, those who succeed in the South as well as the North, are fast and proficient in cutting through the local context. They are keen to detect what is different from what they've known or seen before, and don't allow their perceptual lenses to filter out differences that conflict with their existing rules of thumb. To the contrary, they catch themselves when they subconsciously revert to their old assumptions. They connect with a range of people from substantially different cultural, social, and governmental contexts. They learn to work in the less structured, less predictable environment of the South, where governments can change policies overnight or competitors with cozy ties to customers, suppliers, and regulators can sabotage plans. They're humble and contain their egos. They win trust and confidence from headquarters by providing high-frequency information flows about the local context and by delivering on commitments, and they energize their teams and organizations.

That's how a leader like Manoj Kohli of Bharti Airtel (see page 141) can manage seventeen different countries despite the unique social, economic, and governmental characteristics of each. When Kohli led the India operations, Bharti Airtel was successful using the rule of thumb that if you greatly lower the price of telecom service, you will create huge demand—more usage per customer and enormous numbers of new customers—and thus total revenues will increase. It was successful against competitors, most of which achieved higher revenues through higher prices extracted from a smaller customer base. As Kohli went to each of the seventeen African countries and learned the local context, he saw that the old rule of thumb—raising revenues by offering new services and dropping prices to expand the customer base—did not apply to some of them. The demographics made it harder to get more usage per customer and to bring in large numbers of new customers. The company couldn't just blindly push the old approach. It had to devise a new way to build the business in Africa.

Kohli also recognized the importance of working with a host of unfamiliar regulatory frameworks, local financial and infrastructure institutions, and distribution channels. Actions and priorities—the pace and timing of price changes and introduction of new services, for example— were tailored to the situation and needs of each context. The company was able to recruit almost all its high-level leadership locally, and persuade its ecosystem partners in India to venture into unknown territory to join it in Africa.

THE BASICS

The short list for improving your global leadership capability quickly is to focus on and practice the following, each of which I'll discuss in more detail later in this chapter:

- Rapidly master the local context.
- Create a tangible vision.
- Challenge your rules of thumb.
- Build your team.
- Mobilize your social organization.

Of course the usual long lists of generic leadership traits come into play. All are important, but integrity is crucial. I use the word to go beyond ethics and morality to include delivering what you commit to, saying what you mean, and being skillful when communicating with people in your social networks so you don't make promises you can't keep. There are social networks behind the scenes that you might never know about, where people will verify your statements or discover contradictions. They'll figure out if you're telling the truth or saying one thing to one person and a different thing to someone else. They'll see if you're delivering what you said you would, and whether you're dodging conflicts with headquarters rather than confronting them. Repetition and consistency build trust, and that's what you'll need in order to learn what's really happening. So establishing integrity is a huge positive for your success.

I will start the journey by showing these "soft skills" in action. Consider how leaders in three different positions apply them as they move from North to South: a manager moving into a broader opportunity in the South; a leader at headquarters managing a line of business on a world-wide basis; and the CEO of a business.

ESSENTIAL CHALLENGES FOR
A LEADER MOVING FROM THE
NORTH TO THE SOUTH

As a rising leader working in the home market of your business, you succeeded because you developed a way to find the right balance, the right focus, and the right priorities. You delivered results while growing accustomed to being accountable without having the total authority or necessary resources under your command. You not only succeeded but helped others do so as well, specifically by learning how to work cross-functionally—getting people to collaborate with you and at times exchanging resources, sometimes without a quid pro quo. You're comfortable in this company and this industry, even if growth has only been in the 2 percent to 3 percent range. But you are looking for a challenge and opportunity for personal growth, and one day you get it in spades: Your boss calls you in to tell you he would like you to run the company's India unit, the company's fastest-growing geographic market. It means relocating to Delhi for up to four years.

It's a huge opportunity, but one also fraught with complications. There are career concerns, especially the "out of sight, out of mind" syndrome: Will you be forgotten by key people if you move eight thousand miles from headquarters? You remember the going-away party several years ago for your close friend Elizabeth, who took a position at her company as product development manager in Pune, India. At the party and before, she was teased that she was crazy to go there. People reminded her that the United States was still the largest market, where new ideas were initiated and cutting-edge technological innovation was being developed, and where the depth of technological talent resides. "Besides, Elizabeth," her colleagues said, "you've never lived outside the U.S. It's tough over there. You'd be much better off staying put."

Then there are the personal issues. What will your husband think? He's a success in his own right as a mechanical engineer. Even if he agrees to go, will he be able to continue his career? What about schooling for your kids?

But since you pride yourself on always looking at the facts, you put these concerns momentarily aside. You see a world that is tilting from North to South, specifically the reality that as of 2012, 46 percent of the earnings of S&P 500 companies now originate outside of the United States, a number that will only increase in the future. Moreover, looking further out, the United States, now the dominant market, will be a smaller part of a larger pie, and some positions at so-called headquarters will have shifted from North to South. In fact, it's already happened at companies like P&G, which has shifted the headquarters for its personal-care line of business from Cincinnati to Singapore. You recall the old line from hockey great Wayne Gretzky: "I skate to where the puck is going to be, not where it has been." Over the long run, every business goes where the markets are, to those places where it can create shareholder value and where it can find the resources it needs—human talent as well as natural resources it can depend on. You suspect the time to make the leap is now, before it is too late.

The logic and the facts are there, and you've seen how prescient Elizabeth was. Her colleagues didn't see what was coming—a reduced number of senior-level posts like vice president at the home base and promotions going to those who had significant global experience. By going to a market where the growth was, Elizabeth developed herself and thereby was better positioned for future opportunities— both inside her company and outside it if she ever decides to leave.

You realize that both the local and the national context of this new job in Delhi will be completely different from your job leading a single product line based in the United States. While you're now the global leader of a $200 million product line that's part of a $1 billion global business unit, your job is narrow in its business scope but geographically broad. Now you will be going to a critical country to head the total business unit there. You'll be focused on only one geographic market with sales half what you're in charge of now—just $100 million—but you'll be responsible for all three product lines. You'll have to carry out the *core* of your leadership work—dissecting and reformulating the moneymaking recipe, deciding what to do, and then getting it done—without relying on old rules of thumb. The work content will be different. The competition is different, resource allocation is different, and the number of variables you'll have to deal with is different, perhaps greatly so.

You wonder whether you have what it takes to succeed, so you take a personal inventory. Do I have the motivation and drive to actively search for, listen to, and comprehend what is different from what I have known and has made me successful? Can I make the changes I will need to make? Do I have the temperament to deal with multiple unreliable governments and poor infrastructure?

You've heard some of your friends talk about moving to another country as students or volunteers. They found it exciting and mentally challenging to learn about the community and build the trust of the people, who were both intelligent and eager to work for a better life. You've always envied their sense of adventure. And now, as you think about having to master the ins and outs of the people, the sources of information, the formal and informal power structures, the "way things are done around here" in a new, unique place, you think, *What could be more exciting?*

You recognize that you will have to override many of your familiar rules of thumb, but that's fine. You're one of those people who enjoy breaking through mental barriers to sharpen their perceptual ability. You've always tried to "look around corners" to see what was coming without any preconceived expectations. You're prepared to develop new ways of acting, thinking, and making decisions.

You realize that you may get off balance at first as you grapple with cultural differences. It won't be as easy to get the kind of information you rely on to make managerial decisions in the North. You'll have to learn the social norms that affect information sharing, both vertically and horizontally, especially among your direct reports and one level below. Connecting with people will be important to engendering trust and getting into the information flow—something executives from New York, Munich, or Tokyo typically struggle with.

Loyalty is a much bigger deal in the South. People are loyal to those in power—sometimes overly so—and vice versa. Fidelity to the person rather than the organization is a centuries-old cultural phenomenon. Promotions are often made on the basis of seniority, loyalty to a higher-level person, or invisible social networks. As a result, it's hard to tell if a subordinate is being candid or just aiming to please. While it's natural to gravitate to those who can communicate quickly and clearly and who think like you, you'd have to guard against the tendency to go with those who seem simpatico because they speak your language. You'll have to gauge whether a person truly agrees with you or is saying yes merely out of politeness and a desire to please you. You'll search for competent people who are willing to give you the real information and have the courage to tell you unwelcome facts and truths. That will mean linking with the local social networks and building trust and personal credibility within them.

Many local CEOs, entrepreneurs, and industrialists have deeply ingrained business acumen. Many who have had no formal professional education are extremely bright and are fast thinkers who developed their business savvy early through work experience in their family shops, a trait common in most countries of Asia. They may not have your wide worldview, but their understanding of the business may be broader. They typically understand the total anatomy of moneymaking in a business—the relationships between variables such as cost, turnover, profit, and cash flow, for example—better than functionally trained leaders in the North. You would want to figure out a way to motivate and retain them. On the other hand, some of the local university-trained managers—who are also bright, fast thinkers—rely on basic theories they have learned and speak in generalities. It would be smart to distinguish those who can deliver from those who just talk in theory and generalities.

THE DILEMMA FOR A LEADER
MANAGING A WORLDWIDE LINE
OF BUSINESS

Working out of company headquarters, you have P&L responsibility for a sizable global business unit. The company's goal is to achieve higher growth in revenues, margins, and market share in key countries of the South. At the same time, the slow-growing but larger markets of the North still produce most of the earnings, resulting in a tension of resource allocation: Short-term investments in the South—whose payoff is far away—could reduce total worldwide earnings.

Long-standing habits may have conditioned you to tilt toward the existing markets, since getting the best bang for the buck right now is the norm in corporate America. (And quite possibly, unless your CEO is on the ball and sees the need for change, your key performance indicators, KPIs, will be geared to this outcome.) But the company's future, and yours, depends on your willingness to take risks in long-term strategic locations, which are highly uncertain and subject to the vagaries of local governments.

One reason you have this job is the CEO's confidence that you have the cognitive bandwidth to comprehend the worldwide factors of the business through lenses other than your own and the ability to crystallize what matters and when it matters. You both realize that shifting the center of gravity from North to South represents a major change in the psyche of the people in the business. So you start thinking through the difference between managing a worldwide business in a traditional way and managing on a global basis.

You will need to deal with the ingrained feeling— among your colleagues and possibly in yourself—that "you've been there" and therefore know it all because you've taken several trips a year to key countries in the South. Those short visits are superficial, yet people at global headquarters overrely on them. People in the North have all the power in approving decisions about investments, processes, and procedures in critical areas such as pricing and advertising; they discount the insights of executives living on the scene.

In the new markets of the South, people with local information and knowledge are critical to your decision making. You need to motivate them; you need to pay attention to their judgments; you need to trust them and build their trust in you; and you need to be sensitive to the huge cultural distance between headquarters and the local context of these countries. It's not a challenge to be underestimated. Your headquarters people will need to know that when they visit a country of critical importance, they will have to invest about nine days—two weekends and five working days—to be able to get into the local social circuits. Most executives who are experienced in the global game have already learned this.

While the ingredients of business (margin, cash flow, cost structure, revenue and revenue growth, market share, return on capital, capital intensity, and brand share) are the same in all countries, how they combine and get prioritized is conditioned by the local context. Conflicts between the global and the local goals, especially in the areas of pricing and product development, often arise in operationalizing a worldwide strategy for a line of business. For example, when the same product is intended to be used in several geographies, will you need to change the specifications to produce a lower-priced version for some markets?

In other cases, localizing a global strategy comes down to organizational decisions. Say a company that makes high-quality laminated-wood furniture for Northern markets is heading south. It uses a specialized sales force in the North, which it built over many years. Creating a new sales force in the South will take too long, so the company decides to line up local distributors. That means putting those distributors through an intensive education program before they can effectively market the furniture.

Or, to take on a real mind-bender, say you're a pharmaceuticals company that wants to introduce one of your drugs to a part of Africa. It's priced high in America and somewhat lower in Europe, and those margins are important to paying a return on many years of research and development. The drug is needed in Africa, but you would have to price it much lower. In today's transparent world, there'd be no hiding that discrepancy. How do you ensure your company's financial health while satisfying customers in vastly different economies?

Other tensions are apt to arise when you're adding high-level talent overseas—for example, when you're recruiting a vice chairman of an $80 billion Indian company to join you as the chief executive for Asia and Africa for the most promising category of the business. Compensation and status for such an appointment in the South are usually at the level of a vice president of a North-based business unit. You'll have to fight with headquarters to get this executive into the circle of corporate officers, distinctly above the level of a vice president in a North-based business unit. It will require your best skills of persuasion to quiet the grumbling at headquarters, but that's just part of your new game.

How do you balance the money and people resources you invest to meet worldwide goals with the need to nurture markets and geographic subsegments to position them for the long term? Deciding on the right balance requires savvy resource allocation and goal setting. Procter & Gamble found that it had to rebalance when it tried to expand too widely and too fast in emerging markets. It pulled back to forty product markets that account for 70 percent of its profits.

You have to be able to look beyond the numbers in evaluating and rewarding people to take into account how the numbers are being achieved and what is being built for the future. That means judging how well people are collaborating and how tough the external conditions are. But people need to know that the judgments are not arbitrary, so you have to communicate the basis of your thinking.

THE CEO: POSITIONING THE TOTAL COMPANY TO BE IN TUNE WITH THE TILT

As the CEO of a company expanding into the South, your challenge is vast. The issues are considerably more numerous and complex than those you faced when the business was narrowly focused on a core competency and a relatively small number of well-understood markets. Determining the content of your strategy starts with your view of the big picture—looking from the outside in, future back. You have to be incisive in cutting through the clutter, complexity, and unknowns to see the unstoppable trends. You have to imagine the chess game, then find a path in it, and do so with enough specificity that you can move forward confidently and maybe even make a strategic bet.

Your strategy has to answer questions about where to focus in the South and what changes to make in the North. Part of this strategy-making process is determining which mix of businesses to keep, which to emphasize more, which to shed, and which new ones to add—in line with your outside-in, future-back viewpoint and suppressing the contemporary practice of looking inside out. You have to have a clear fix on your present and future competition, from budding but ambitious local competitors to well-established multinationals and perhaps some players that are backed by their governments. You have to find the right balance between the North and the South, between the short and long term, and shift that balance as the tilt evolves. This will challenge your attitude toward risk taking.

Imagine that you're making a presentation to the board of directors to get their approval to invest half a billion dollars in China over the next five years. The board is not enthusiastic. The nonexecutive chairman of the board asks you and your management team who in your industry makes money in China and which global competitors are moving in quickly. "When does management see meeting the cost of capital in China's high-wage-inflation environment and under uncertain government behavior?" he adds. Another director chimes in: "Isn't the basic question whether we should even go into China? It will be well into the future before it's the world's largest market, and we know that we won't make money for a long time. Are we better off staying in the geographies we know, making money and creating shareholder value?"

A third director notes that because of the industry you're in, you'll be in competition with the Chinese government. The Chinese government wants the latest technology now and in the future and expects you to be a minority partner, running your total global business from China. It's a thorny dilemma: the choice between becoming number one in a larger market with all the headaches of a minority shareholder and allowing someone else to take that spot and become a bigger competitor than you in the future. Are you willing to make a strategic bet? If the board resists, is it because they don't see what you see?

Unfortunately, the above is real dialogue from a board meeting I attended; the board was the biggest impediment to the company's taking advantage of the global tilt. As CEO, you need to provide a clear view of the global tilt landscape and its unstoppable trends (see Chapter 2) to help the board understand what's at stake. You need to work closely with them to bring them up to speed on the nature of the South, because most boards are not well versed in its nuances and vagaries. The impression they get from their peers in the North is that it's hard to make money in the South. You might want to arrange trips for them to spend some time in the South—more time than the typical short, highly packed visits that leave very little informal time to soak up the local conditions and get engaged in the social system. You might even want to do what some boards do: Schedule a meeting in the South. Have directors stay for a week along with their spouses and create opportunities for them to connect socially with influential local people. That will give them a personal, up-close understanding of how things work there.

There is no way around the fact that as a CEO, many fate-changing decisions lie before you. You have no choice but to tackle them head-on. GE CEO Jeff Immelt created a list of ten key decisions he had to make. I borrowed that concept to create a set of questions that any CEO should consider before embarking on a quest to go south.

THE TEN DECISIONS OF A CEO

Take a clean sheet of paper and answer these questions:

1. Which executives and teams will participate in shaping the strategy, deciding how to operationalize it, and leading the change in its execution?

2. What is your new strategy and its road map? What will the company not do, what shifts are intended to be made from the present, and which parts of your existing strategy will be jettisoned or deemphasized?

3. What shift will you make in capital allocation? What will be its timing? What financial and people resources need to be shifted—extracted from the North and redeployed in the South—to keep overhead and other costs from bloating?

4. What new capabilities will be required? For example, will the company need a different approach to logistics? What capabilities are no longer relevant?

5. How will you redesign the content, location, and outcomes of operating mechanisms—specifically the financial and

talent reviews? For example, should reviews of a worldwide line of business take place in China?

6. How does the content of information and its architecture have to change?

7. What decisions need to be made where? What shifts need to take place? Which people from the South need to be a critical part of corporate decision making?

8. Should you change the organizational structure? If so, when, and how?

9. What KPIs, quantitative and qualitative, will drive the new game, and which old ones need to go? Can they be changed midstream?

10. What will be the content, frequency, and media to create excitement about this change internally and externally? Positive external communications often influence the psychology of the workforce.

A savvy CEO thinks through the sequencing of such decisions and evaluates their second-, third-, and fourth-order consequences. Decisiveness matters. Analysis paralysis can kill you.

CHALLENGES COMMON TO ALL LEVELS OF LEADERSHIP

The sea change in attitude, behavior, and skills required in a tilted world is important not only for those making the transition to a posting in a totally new environment but also for those who remain in the home market. Understanding the particular issues of moving from North to South will help any leader perform better, whether a CEO, a business-unit or profit-and-loss manager, the leader of a business function such as HR, finance, or compliance, or an operating manager of the supply chain or global branding. It will also help leaders in the South as they move from one Southern country to another or from the South to the North.

RAPIDLY MASTER THE LOCAL CONTEXT

No matter what your level of responsibility, there are certain behavioral basics that you need to understand and master when you go south, because your soft skills will greatly affect your ability to make good decisions. Let me explain.

A person from the South—from, say, India, China, Brazil, Indonesia, or Nigeria—coming to America has an easier time understanding the market than vice versa. America has more reliable sources of information and top-notch consultants, so knowledge, information, and expert judgment are readily available. It is relatively easy for new-comers to move. It also helps that a significant portion of leaders from the South (or their associates) have been educated in or worked in the North. They know what is available and whom to rely on. Those factors, combined with experience in the South, make a potent combination.

Going from America or Europe to, say, China is much tougher. Being a good listener and valuing local people is crucial. In India, for example, local CEOs know that each of the thirty states is like a country unto itself in terms of consumer behavior, segmentation, infrastructure, and lo-gistics. Often the most crucial part is understanding how decisions get made and how information flows among the various participants. You have to build social networks and learn how multiple government agencies and levels of government interact with one another and what the con-nections are to your industry.

Avoid the trap that many leaders going from the United States, Europe, and Japan fall into by mixing largely in social networks of their own kind. In most countries of the South, where information can be elusive and unreli-able, you will need to connect with people who can interpret it knowledgeably and provide accurate qualitative judgments. Build a social network by finding mentors or creating an advisory group of people who can educate you about the anatomy, reality, and context of decision making by local authorities. Don't try to rush it; in many cases, you may have to be less efficient to be more effective. The "let's hurry up and get on with the job" mentality is not conducive to building the cohesion and trust that inform a social network.

As you listen to local people, you need to have your mental computer running to become conscious of the person's frame of reference. Social norms around sharing information may differ from those inside your company. Unless you spend enough time to build social cohesion, you might not get to the truth. You need to fish out what the person has in mind and repeat and reconfirm before you finish the conversation. Be patient and work at it. In many of these cultures, follow-through is lacking. You need to have follow-through. As you practice this, you will learn the culture and social norms of the players.

Drilling to the specifics of a particular country should complement, not substitute for, your outside-in, future-back view of the external landscape. You should continually practice sorting through the complexity of external change, selecting what matters, and identifying business opportunities. Test your courage to make strategic bets and investments where some factors are unknowable. Create your own daily, weekly, or monthly routine to detect global forces that will change the game.

CREATE A TANGIBLE VISION

If your people, your partners, and your customers in the South are going to take you seriously, you must make your vision *tangible* and *communicable*. It must be shaped with the participation of your key people, since the process of shaping builds commitment and buy-in. To be credible it must have clear milestones; lofty visions will be seen as hallucinations. You should communicate your vision relentlessly and repetitively, ensuring that the recipients get the content the way it was intended and that they are committed to it.

For example, when Bharti Airtel took charge of Zain's operations in fifteen African countries, the business had had five different owners over the previous decade and its people were (understandably) skeptical about how long the new owner would stick around. Within the first week, the company got its top one hundred African leaders together to create a common vision. It took a week of working together to iron it out. Manoj Kohli, with his HR background, is a master of facilitation, and the week provided ample time to get to know each person. There was plenty of dialogue, and he is a listener par excellence, a precise thinker, and a great communicator with an ability to connect with people from all kinds of cultures.

The vision they created is that "Bharti will be the most loved brand in the daily lives of African people by 2015." This vision is tangible, measurable, and time based. It is consumer focused and subliminal, planting the notion of "love" rather than "like," and it is in contrast with other brands. The word "loved" implies continuity with the consumer in delivering desirable services, and at the same time focuses the one hundred people on doing everything they can and must do to get consumers to love the brand. They in turn will get their organizations pointing toward the same goal.

Kohli returned after two weeks to talk with people and ensure that they understood the content of the vision and the direction the company would take. He learned how the hundred people were shaping specific plans to pursue the direction and execute.

A vision that is tangible and measurable and linked to business priorities helps execution by pointing employees and partners in the same direction. Meeting specific benchmarks creates energy. To convert Bharti Airtel's vision into reality, employees and partners focus on two business imperatives: affordable prices and a compelling service offering. Management focuses on decisions such as what services are to be offered and at what pace in each country, what infrastructure will be built and at what pace, what investments will be made and executed on time and on budget, and finally, what will be the criteria for selection and promotion of talent to bring *extraordinary managerial intensity* to accomplish the vision by 2015.

CHALLENGE YOUR
RULES OF THUMB

In almost all cases, leaders going into a new territory will have to tweak if not radically change their intuitive, well-tested rules of thumb. These can be especially damaging if you try to use them with people in the South who can't relate to the specifics of your previous context. You will need resilience and psychological flexibility to learn new ones, modify some old ones, and kill others. Take just two examples:

- Consumers: In the North you know where your consumers shop, what information they get beforehand, and what price they'll pay. They go to large retail stores or buy online, they get discount coupons or notices of sales, and they use digital media to comparison shop. By contrast, most consumers in

the South buy in small shops with low margins, which
are served by more than one layer of intermediate
distributors. You need to study the system to
understand how it differs from your rules of thumb.

- Competitors: Most rules of thumb for understanding
  competitive behavior will be dead wrong in the South.
  Competitors in the South manage for cash, not for
  profit, and work on very thin margins, high velocity
  of assets, and skimpy overhead. They are generally not
  publicly held, so they don't hire accounting firms and
  internal auditors and aren't bound by SEC-type rules.
  They are driven by market share, not market value. As
  a result they are decisive, fast, and entrepreneurial.

BUILD YOUR TEAM

A common challenge for leaders is to leverage the organization's global scale and scope and worldwide talent pool
to carry out key initiatives that either create new value or
create differentiation against competitors, be they local or
multinational. Such projects as development of software,
integrating intellectual capital from research and development sites spread across the globe, and redesigning global
supply chains are often designed and executed by teams of
people working across functions and countries and business

units. Successfully building these teams is a critical weapon for winning in the changing landscape of the tilt.

Leaders who do this well are what I call *global integrators*—a new term for a new kind of leader. An integrator's skill is to build trust among people from very different cultures and disciplines. What helps is to work at ensuring that they know the end goal very precisely and have the same understanding of the information, data, facts, and external context. A global integrator works with people individually and collectively, tapping their knowledge and expertise in searching out the right solutions and getting each of them to modify their view to get to the common end point. This is repetitive work for a leader. A one-time iteration will not get you there.

MOBILIZE YOUR SOCIAL ORGANIZATION

Execution of any vision, change, or initiative requires that you energize the people in your organization and point them toward the specific actions they need to take.

Here's your checklist:

- Ensure that communication—top down and bottom up—is filter free. It should be like blood flowing freely through the arteries of the organization.

- Simplify decision making and accountability. If decisions are not being executed and goals not being achieved, get to the root cause to see if the factors are controllable.

- Get to know the natural talent, experiences, and judgments of key players as well and rapidly as you can, and put them in the right places. Evaluate how well people and their jobs are matched. Is there a deficiency of skills needed to achieve the vision? Deal with the issues that arise in melding different cultures. Differences in information sharing are common: When Mark Fields, now the executive at Ford in charge of North and South America, went to Ford's Japanese partner in 1997–98, he quickly pinpointed the need for a major shift in a culture where information was compartmentalized. The managers were functional experts who didn't understand the business as a whole. As Fields explains, "If the manufacturing person produced the number of units that he was supposed to produce, then the company should have profits. Or if the head of purchasing achieved his objectives for the year, his assumption was that the business was in good shape. The business was never put together for them so that they could see how each of their pieces added up to a corporate whole." After making clear his expectation that people should be more open, Fields took them to an off-site meeting to learn about one another's functions and form a common view of the business as a whole. He stipulated that they would speak only Japanese, with interpreters when necessary. Speaking in their native language would make them more comfortable and allow the nuances and feelings to come through, so the exchange of information and views would be more accurate. After two days during which Fields continually asked questions to draw them out, the individuals began to see things from a broader perspective and came to appreciate why they should be more forward about sharing information.

- Build credibility and trust by doing what you say, sharing both good and bad news, explaining clearly the rationale for your decisions.

- Resolve any tension with headquarters. This is not a one-shot deal; tension will always be there. Say you're a local business-unit manager and you see a huge opportunity to make strategic bets. You know the local context much better than your global manager several thousand miles away. He has never lived or worked in the South and gets his information from industry experts, occasional assignments he has given to consultants, and you. Your ability to make your bets depends on whether you can get him to accept your judgment. Prepare yourself with rigorous analysis and explicit delineation of the risks under a range of conditions to persuade him that your assessment of the local context justifies the required investment. Be sure the proposed return justifies those risks. Also, be prepared to work your way through the layers of decision making and to correct distortions in information. Build trust and confidence in yourself by communicating vigorously with the decision makers, creating a high frequency of information flow about your plan and its implications for the business, so that over time they come to see that your finger is on the pulse and you have good judgment.

Reorienting an entire business to succeed in the tilt is akin to performing a heart transplant: the surgeon has to keep her patient alive while cutting and splicing. For a business, the challenge is keeping the company smoothly functional and delivering the numbers amid the trauma. Next I'll take you into the corporate operating theater, where you will see how to do it.

CHAPTER SIX

SHIFTING POWER, RESOURCES, AND BEHAVIOR

THE ORGANIZATION IN A TILTED WORLD

P reparing the organization to execute your new strategy requires at least as much thinking as creating the strategy in the first place. Your goal is a fast, adaptable organization that can dance to the different tempo of the tilted world. Organizations have to be able to respond instantly to the changing external context, win in the local market, and also build capabilities for the future. Local leaders have to be empowered with authority and resources so they can move without losing time waiting for the approval of a distant headquarters.

Facing changes of such magnitude, leaders typically assume they'll have to start by redoing the organizational structure. This is not something to look forward to: it can be excruciatingly difficult to execute; it can drain energy and disrupt business during the transition from the old to the new structure.

There's an alternative that is almost certainly more effective: Focus first on the organization's social system, the other half of the equation. Wherever human beings work together, their behaviors and actions (or inactions) form a social system. The guts of the social system are how its people and groups interact and make decisions—how information gets shared among whom, how tradeoffs get made and by whom, and whether behavior in those interactions creates energy or drains it. I have observed that skillfully changing the social system can accomplish what's needed. So powerful is the impact of the social system that sometimes it's all the change that's needed.

Three organizational shifts are essential for you to take advantage of the tilt: shifts in *power* (what decisions will be made, by whom, with what input, and where in the organization), *resources* (leaders, experts, and funding), and *behavior* (attitudes, habits, and rules of thumb). If you are the top leader, you can drive these shifts through your focused, disciplined use of tools and mechanisms you most likely already use—for example, using the budgeting process to ensure that resources are directed toward growth areas in the South, or incorporating in performance reviews a person's openness to inputs from people in the

South. If you're an upper or middle manager, you need to know what changes to make, how to cope with the inherent tensions they create, how your work content and time allocation will change, and what personal habits you have to adopt to make them happen.

Making these shifts in the social system first will actually help you make a better decision about what type of organizational structure you need. You'll be able to judge what skills and expertise—and therefore *who*—should be in decision-making roles and who has become a roadblock. When people experience good results without the discontinuity of abrupt change in reporting structures, they are more open to further adjustments. The transition is smoother because they will see the logic of the change and the organization's dominant psychology will have shifted. One CEO told me that after power, resources, and behavior had begun to move, the organization wanted to know why the change in organizational structure was taking so long.

True, changing the structure first has advantages that some leaders will find compelling. It's easier to bring new blood into key positions, and the changes in decision making, budgets, capital allocations, and KPIs can be executed all at once. The transition usually takes about six months. But during that time many people become confused and conflicted. When one large U.S. multinational recently undertook a major restructuring, some talent left for greener pastures, and some middle-level managers told me that working with people who did not yet know what they were doing in their new jobs was torture. Relationships had to be built anew, internally and externally, with partners.

Leaders who want to attend to the social system first must exercise the ultimate in intellectual honesty in making their organization fit to meet the emerging challenge. Fit means having the capability and/or systems to find and pursue the opportunities in the tilt and, equally important, the psychology to win. A practical, time-effective way to assess fitness is assembling a team of people to include HR, finance, and legal, and scheduling a retreat to address the following questions:

1. Is your talent pool in the South strong and deep enough?

2. Do your budgets reflect your growth priorities?

3. Do KPIs and compensation reflect the changes you're trying to make?

4. Where are the blockages in the flow of know-how, technology, and expertise?

5. Are your people, your budget, and your business reviews helping you make the shift?

6. Are critical decisions being made in the right way?

Answers to these questions will point you toward actions that need to be taken. There's no universal set, but the actions must be clear, specific, and communicable to the people who will implement them. Then you as a leader must focus intensely on execution: assigning clear accountability, following through, and celebrating accomplishments. Rigorous, disciplined follow-through is imperative to keep people from reverting to old behaviors.

1.

IS YOUR TALENT POOL IN THE SOUTH STRONG AND DEEP ENOUGH?

Your selection and assignment of top leaders in the South is crucial, not just the head of the country, region, or business unit but also the CFO, head of human resources, and the compliance officer. Having strong, competent leaders who share your company's values paves the way for shifts in power and resources by ensuring that those things are in good hands.

When Bharti Airtel CEO Sunil Mittal contemplated the African acquisition, he realized that the risk was high due to the challenge of taking on many different countries at once and the high debt the company would incur. Ineffective execution would be a disaster. But he had in Manoj Kohli a leader with the experience, values, and skills to take on the task. Kohli had the ability to see the big picture while understanding the various country contexts, including their governments.

Many companies make one of two mistakes in appointing a leader to drive growth in the promising Southern markets they've chosen. The first is sending a person who's too low level and/or too narrow in perspective—for example, a person who is superb in his function but oblivious to the broader implications of his work. These people have trouble seeing the bigger picture of the business and might not pick up the nuances of making money in a different country. One company sent a leader from Brazil to head its business in Indonesia, but while he was a technical wiz and had performed well in his home country, he didn't have the broad perspective of a businessperson. Equally damaging, he couldn't abandon his old rules of thumb about the political environment and could not build relationships with key people in the government. The fact that many leaders are sent to jobs in growth markets for only two or three years before being reposted compounds the problem, because such frequent turnover makes it hard to build relationships. The local competitor who has business savvy and long-term relationships will have an edge. Whomever you choose must have the skills, personality, and mind-set to compete against locals who may think big and who may be aggressive, highly entrepreneurial, accustomed to living on low margins, and well connected with high-level people in that country.

It may be hard to pull one of your strongest leaders out of a job in the North, because you feel that you need to preserve your strength or contend with tough issues in markets that still generate the lion's share of cash, revenue, and earnings. You don't want to jeopardize your annual performance in the home market. Moreover, those leaders you would like to assign might hesitate to move for fear that they'll become second-class citizens and fall off the radar for promotions. Concerns that you'll lose the best performers and people you depend on most makes it more comfortable to assign lower-level people to those growth posts in the South. You will need to explicitly reassure your best leaders that performing well in those jobs can put them in the succession pool, provided the term is longer than, say, two years. Former GE CEO Jack Welch put Jim McNerney in Hong Kong for five years. McNerney became one of the three contenders to replace Jack Welch, and went on to become CEO of 3M and then Boeing.

Opening leadership jobs in the North can be a great motivator and developmental opportunity for up-and-coming talent.

An obvious alternative is to hire a local leader who knows the local context. But you should avoid a mistake companies often make: hiring one who is not of high enough caliber. You need, in the language of business leaders of the South, a big guy. The perennial challenge of hiring the right person gets tougher when the environment is unfamiliar and the competition for top talent is fierce. But it makes all the difference in the world and thus requires that the CEO and head of HR devote whatever time and energy are needed to get it right.

Recruiting and reference-checking high-caliber leaders in the high-growth South may be more challenging than in the North. You'll find plenty of people with impressive degrees but far fewer who can carry out the responsibilities of a business leader. Headhunters and advisory boards can help you find people and check their backgrounds. And your company's good reputation will attract them, particularly if it's known for helping people develop their talents. You'll need people who are masters of the local context and have social contacts, along with having business acumen and values that fit your company. And remember that verifiable operating experience is not the same as a track record of execution.

Nothing overcomes having the wrong leadership. It's hard enough to relinquish power from headquarters. If top management doesn't trust the competence of local leaders, the power shift is not going to happen. Decisions will be reviewed and second-guessed, slowing the local organization's responsiveness, and resources will be withheld for fear that they'll be misspent. Other people will pick up on your hesitation and be less receptive to the leader's inputs, ideas, and information. Replacing the leader later wastes precious time.

Leaders in the South will expect to be compensated at levels that approach those in the North, usually with more fringe benefits. The best talent simply won't accept the old local levels. The bigger tussle is that many of them want to be corporate officers and not just an officer of the national subsidiary or business unit. They want big titles such as vice chairman and expect to be compensated accordingly. Many of the best leaders will be coming from very senior positions in large organizations locally, including other entrenched multinationals, and will be well attuned to any subtle signals that their career paths will be limited. To join your company, they have to see that they will be important players in a diverse global talent pool: part of the senior team and under consideration for bigger jobs in the future. Companies such as GE, Honeywell, Unilever, and Siemens provide a rich value proposition for such leaders because their systems ensure that such people can advance to jobs with broader responsibilities, including big ones at headquarters. At GE, for example, they interact directly with vice chairman John Rice, who lives in Hong Kong. They sit in the front row at GE's annual management meeting at Boca Raton, Florida.

While you should be open to moving talent from the South to the North, you should expect that leaders assigned to the South will stay in their jobs long enough to build their top team and their own succession. Most teams will be a mix of expats and local people recruited from diverse companies. A crucial task for the leader is to recruit and retain this group and get them working together better than the local competition.

As you recruit or appoint high-caliber leaders, particularly for your highest-priority growth markets in the South, you need to be sure that your top leaders in the South, whether recruited locally or drawn from the home base, are not constrained by too many layers of reporting and do not feel buried by having to get multiple approvals. For leaders of the most critical countries—those with huge potential that will affect the destiny of the company— a direct line to the CEO may be best. Some companies have abolished regional headquarters, organizing instead by clusters based on geographic proximity. At GE, leaders in a cluster report to a vice chairman and interact directly with the CEO every six weeks.

Streamlined reporting relationships speed the responsiveness to local competition, avoid distortions in the flow of information, and also signal the importance of the position, which affects recruiting and retention. They also open people's minds at headquarters. It's universal that people want their voices to be heard. The CEO or whoever is conducting meetings and discussions can send strong signals about the value of a leader's perspective by listening carefully, drawing the person out if necessary, and relying on his or her judgment. It's largely through such discussions that trust and respect develop and behavior begins to shift. (All of that is predicated, of course, on having recruited a leader whose abilities are up to the task and whose values are in line with the rest of the company.)

Boosting the caliber and role of leaders in critical markets of the South has serious, sometimes painful ramifications for the North. You can't continually increase the number of company officers—vice presidents, executive vice presidents, vice chairmen, and the like. Many will either have to move to another part of the world or be asked to leave. One way to look at it is to consider how many of your top leaders are from countries in the South. If you have, say, fifty officer-level leaders, all of whom are based in the North, and your strategy is to expand in the South, you might want at least ten officers from high-growth countries. The question then is whether you can really afford to increase the total number from fifty to sixty or will need to reduce the number of officers in the North. Even among your markets in the North, you might have to reassign and resize your leadership. Should you continue to devote the same level of human resources to Portugal, Spain, or Italy, for example, given their economic problems? Maybe some people should be shifted to Germany, because it has become critical to winning in Europe and the Middle East. You also have to be honest about whether the leaders in the North will buy into the organizational changes you're trying to make, because they likely control a lot of resources.

Inevitably there will be a morale problem. You'll lose some of your colleagues and some very talented, dedicated, and successful employees. You'll be accused of being cold-hearted and perhaps even unpatriotic. You're not, but Wall Street is clear: reduce cost, cut overhead, and put resources in growth markets and at the same time deliver TSR. What's more, avoiding these problems is just as dismal as facing them: bloated head count in a slow-growth environment tends to spur internal politics and backstabbing.

2.

DO YOUR BUDGETS REFLECT YOUR
GROWTH PRIORITIES?

Senior leaders need to develop greater awareness of the social and political aspects of budgeting, a central tool in shifting resources. With that comes a shift in power, and the budgeting process itself changes behavior. Too often, though, resource allocation has the opposite effect: preserving existing power bases and reinforcing the status quo. It's done on a retrospective basis, not a prospective one. Those who control these decisions have outdated assumptions that prevent them from seeing what needs to be done. Or if they're able to make the intellectual connection between the change in strategy and the new allocation of resources, the human side gets in the way of acting on it. Let's face it: people hate to extract resources. They're swayed by psychological factors, such as not wanting to disappoint people they've worked with over time.

Budgets and KPIs are commitments you live or die by. A failure to meet an important target subjects you to embarrassment among your peers, bosses, and team and can affect your pocketbook and chances for promotion, especially when exceeding the KPIs can mean an annual bonus of 200 percent of the target. The budgeting process generates a huge amount of preparation and jockeying. The competition and negotiation is something of an internal game and intensifies when growth is anemic or declining and resources have to be cut back. The managerial tussle comes because there's not enough money to continue to fund the North at the same level and also fuel growth in the South without affecting the results Wall Street looks for. While it's easy to say you want to expand in a growth market, the reality is that resource constraints create fierce tensions around operating budgets.

In many cases leaders in the North are fighting to preserve what they have. They know that without the same level of funding they're used to, they'll have to reduce the number of people on the payroll. That's something every leader dreads, especially when it has to be done surgically. Leaders squirm when people start asking, "Why do I have to go? My performance scorecard is stellar. Why not somebody else?" Closing an entire plant is somehow easier because it's justified on the basis of hard numbers and analytics.

Top managers have their own reasons to keep funding the North at the usual levels: They're concerned about damaging the profit streams it delivers. But adjustments are likely to be necessary even within the North, because some segments will be growing more than others or one market is coming under attack from a global contender.

Leaders in the South are more likely fighting for resources because they see opportunities. But are they good opportunities? What margins will they generate and when? The trick is to recognize that a portion of the operating budget for a growth market in a country in the South is actually a strategic investment that will pay off in years, not months. It takes time to build a sales force from scratch, train a staff, build a brand, and utilize a facility to capacity, and results will be less predictable because of the volatility of macro factors as well as local conditions and competitive dynamics.

One other difference between the North and the South should be taken into account: Leaders in the South may lack experience in the budget game. People who have worked in the company for a long time in entrenched markets will be better able to influence the decision makers by virtue of their proximity to the bosses and the psychological affinity that's developed over time. You as a leader need to be aware of those psychological contracts and know when to intervene. You also have to ensure continuity in budgeting from year to year. Funding the South in fits and starts is a disaster for retaining top talent and winning in the market.

Because resource allocation is a detail-oriented task, many leaders hate it. They think of it as management, not leadership. Yet it is through this nitty-gritty exercise that leaders shape the behaviors and psychology of the organization. A top-down process is faster than bottom-up, and a rolling eight-quarter plan is a good way to build in the flexibility needed to adapt to changing conditions. Budgets can be adjusted quarterly.

To be aligned with the company's growth goals, decisions about capital expenditures should also take into account North/South differences. In the South, these expenditures generally are needed to create something new. In the North, they're usually for maintenance and incremental expansion. Returns are usually higher in the North, and with a faster payback, even though an investment in the South may take the company further against the competition. Skill in setting hurdle rates and risk requirements is critical. Different countries and market segments are in different phases of development and are affected differently by macro conditions. Poor judgment and risk aversion will lead to the North getting the lion's share of investment capital. People will keep doing what they've been doing. Behavior and power won't shift.

Discretionary funds constitute another tool to shape the organizational tilt, one that you may be reluctant to use because of the potential backlash. Say a few months into the budgeting cycle the head of a country unit sees the need for more money outside her operating budget to retain a consulting firm and fund travel and other costs associated with entering a new market. Budgets for the various global lines of business have already been set. Now the CEO has to decide whether to give the country head the additional, say, $50 million being requested. Many headquarters lack the flexibility to adjust. Yet it might make sense to have a certain amount of "risk funds" available to help local leaders seize opportunities or overcome problems as they operationalize the strategy. When business unit leaders presented their two-year plans at one company's planning session, the head of China described his intention to recruit partners because building a sales force from scratch was too expensive. But it became clear after discussion that the sales force was a better route. Realizing that the budget for China didn't allow for it, the CEO insisted that the head of the Asia Pacific region shift the allocations accordingly.

3.

DO KPIs AND COMPENSATION REFLECT
THE CHANGES YOU'RE TRYING TO MAKE?

Shifts in power and behavior are reinforced through frequent, timely feedback on performance. Even if you appraise performance only annually for compensation purposes, you should give feedback more often. Some companies do it quarterly. In tracking performance against goals and KPIs, it's important to remember that conditions in the South change faster and are much less predictable than in the North, and the variability is often beyond the leader's control. You shouldn't sacrifice discipline, but you have to be sure to probe for the reasons behind any misses. I saw a situation in India where the country manager's budget and KPIs became obsolete within months because the country's power plants couldn't get coal and were running at 30 percent to 40 percent of capacity, causing production to wind down. Interest rates had gone up, and so had the debt service. Currency swings, a rise or fall in inflation, a spike in commodity prices—all these things are common in the South yet can affect the unit's profitability beyond the manager's control. Other things, however, are manageable and measurable, such as the impact on market share, cost, and productivity targets.

Recognizing the realities leaders live with in those markets has a tremendous effect on their morale and therefore on both their ability to succeed and the likelihood of retaining them. Any adjustments you make might be perceived as unfair by others in the company, but you can't let that keep you from making adjustments you know are right. You may have to make your rationale explicit to all.

More important than feedback on quantitative factors is feedback on the qualitative ones, such as behavior. This is where you can directly challenge and redirect people's attitudes and actions. Is the technology department sharing its expertise with those in the South? Is the leader of a country in the South getting into the right networks with the government? Are people in the North and South working together to figure out a pricing philosophy that works to capture the market in the South without upsetting customers in other countries? Global organizations must have simplified, standardized processes company-wide, but people don't like changing the systems they're accustomed to. Are they compromising the company's decisiveness and draining energy by resisting this change?

Two types of behavior bear particular watching: collaboration and power sharing. For example, you can see collaboration in the willingness of a global unit or headquarters function to share experts and expertise with people in the South even if doing so affects their own budget. When the company has sophisticated technology and a huge tacit knowledge base at headquarters that the local markets need to tap, phases of that technology transfer should be mapped out. If the demand on resources becomes too great or the transfer of know-how is contentious for legitimate reasons, the collaborative solution is to seek relief from the senior people rather than simply refuse the requests for help. Only competitors can benefit when the issue is allowed to simmer.

Power sharing is observable when, for instance, a leader allows the decision making to take place in the South. If this isn't happening, you should question why the leader has failed to turn decisions over to those who are closer to the market. Maybe the local competence hasn't been upgraded yet, but maybe the leader simply has a psychological block. Such defensive behavior is precisely what prevents many companies from moving faster and better. It cannot go unchecked.

An additional area to watch in the South is values: Is the person demonstrating corporate values and abiding by the company's code of conduct? Compliance is a necessity, not a choice. Site visits give you the opportunity to observe and accumulate evidence to make your appraisals meaningful and accurate.

4.

WHERE ARE THE BLOCKAGES IN THE FLOW OF KNOW-HOW, TECHNOLOGY, AND EXPERTISE?

Everyday business activity is where the money is made and the talent is tested, where strategies and direction are acted on or not. It is where delays can prevent you from meeting your goals in the South, such as winning a pivotal contract investors are counting on. The top leaders can't intervene every time people disagree or fail to cooperate, but they should sample the organization's social system to identify blockages—such as lack of expertise or inflexible leaders in charge of resources—and ensure that there are conflict resolution mechanisms to deal with them. These mechanisms might be as simple as a monthly teleconference presided over by a high-level executive.

Most organizations are structured as a matrix, whether or not they are labeled as such. The matrix is designed to take advantage of the company's scale and at the same time identify anchor points to pin P&L responsibility at lower levels. Those charged with P&L responsibility integrate various factors and make decisions to deliver a business result, such as hitting revenue or market-share targets, generating cash, or earning a certain return on assets. People at the anchor points have accountability but not traditional command-and-control authority or budgetary resources. They can't order people who don't report to them to get things done, but they make sure the agreed-upon numbers are met.

In a matrix, a middle manager usually ends up reporting to two or more bosses. A finance person in Singapore, for instance, reports to his local boss and also to a finance manager at headquarters, who in turn reports to the CFO.

The finance person in Singapore has to get approvals and resources from two chains of command. The finance person at headquarters has to decide how to assign resources among the various people reporting to her, all of whom likely have compelling rationales. The bottom line is that requests for resources may go through filters that unintentionally distort the business case, and decisions are often delayed. That can become a competitive disadvantage against a well-heeled, entrepreneurial, large-scale local competitor.

Those at headquarters who are doling out the support and assigning the experts have to meet their own KPIs, which at most companies are fixed annually and therefore can't accommodate a sudden surge of demand from the South. If they give the South what is being requested, another unit will get less. The decision makers will feel the tension of the matrix, as do the various P&L managers, who have no direct control over some of the resources they need to deliver on their goals.

Competition for scarce resources is a reality. The most crucial need in the South is usually expertise—engineers, maintenance people, manufacturing-process experts, legal and compliance, and human-resources professionals. It's a common complaint that while leaders in the South need to tap corporate talent to grow the business, those who run those functions or departments get the message from their bosses loud and clear: "You can't increase head count." So while leaders in the South are expected to grow the business, they feel they have insufficient human resources to do so. It doesn't help that for cultural reasons leaders in the South might not be as forceful or explicit in advocating for themselves. One country manager expressed the pressure he felt this way: "The CEO keeps increasing the demands on me, but my people are limited. I can't get any relief."

The assignment of expertise is the quandary almost all businesses wrestle with as they try to preserve or expand their presence in the North while tapping into the South's growth markets. Highly specialized experts, such as those in a specific area of process technology or the law, are particularly precious. Misallocation of their time can cause acute bottlenecks to growth. You have to detect the bottlenecks, whether they're organizational (too much demand on expertise amid a head-count freeze) or behavioral (emanating from fear or insecurity). Some middle managers perceive that by transferring know-how to the South they will be building their own competitor and their job will be eliminated at some point. This is especially troubling for people in their fifties, who might feel they're being taken advantage of. Issues of respect for and trust in the leaders in the South and reliability of information also come into play. It takes time to trust someone else's judgment and perceptions; in the meantime, their requests might carry less psychological weight. It's also common for people in the North to question whether leaders in other countries are as committed as they are to the company as a whole. Any doubt creates subconscious resistance to collaboration and sharing.

How do you find out about the blockages? It's usually obvious to people in the middle ranks, who live with these tensions and frustrations. One way for those at the top to detect them is through a pulse survey, a questionnaire that polls the doers, not just the talkers. These are usually done by a third party through interviews in which the tone of voice can come through. Questions about the flow of information, speed of decision making, and formal and informal filters can point to trouble spots within a business function or between people in the local and global units. If the survey exposes some people who refuse to change, you can make heroes of those who are leading. Ideally you should keep the survey consistent so you can track progress over time.

A second way to detect and deal with organizational or behavioral impediments is through a social mechanism, such as a meeting—telephonic or otherwise—at least every six weeks or so of people who need to collaborate in one way or another. GE CEO Jeff Immelt conducts such a meeting every six weeks; P&G CEO Bob McDonald holds one monthly; and Ford CEO Alan Mulally conducts one every week.

It's crucial to ask the right questions in these meetings. The top leaders need to know that the organizational tilt is moving at the right speed and that the company is winning in the areas it's targeted—and if it isn't, why not. Opening with a basic question such as "How are we doing in capturing customers?" immediately opens the door for discussion about the need for senior people from headquarters to help reach the top decision makers in the customer's shop, or to voice concerns about compliance in writing contracts. Similarly, asking, "What's happening on our top-priority project?" creates the opportunity to hear that the technical people have not been transferred yet. The unblocking—and therefore the shifts in behavior, power, and resources—can happen right then and there. Leaders will more easily sniff out the bottlenecks by doing some homework, contemplating what the contentious issues might be, and bringing them front and center. Determining among the group who should do what next makes the solutions and accountability visible to all. Then it's a matter of following up six weeks later, if not before.

A happy by-product of this mechanism is that it builds a common culture. The frequency of the discussions creates a more informal environment. People get to know one another, which is conducive to candor and collaboration, and they see what values and behaviors get reinforced. This mechanism is in fact one of the fastest ways to create a shift in power, resources, and behaviors.

5.

ARE YOUR REVIEWS HELPING YOU MAKE THE SHIFT?

I have given you an inkling of the issues and dilemmas you face as you try to mobilize a large organization to win in the tilt. Time is limited, so be sure you're getting the best return on it. Social mechanisms like the six-week meeting are great expanders of your capacity. Properly designed and led, they can drive organizational change while at the same time ensuring delivery of the quarterly numbers. Monthly operating reviews of a unit or function; quarterly financial reviews; annual strategy, talent, or compliance reviews; and budgeting sessions—all of these are social mechanisms, recurring meetings of a set of people across organizational lines. For simplicity, let's refer to them as reviews.

Every company has a collage of these, and they absorb a huge amount of time and mental energy. A CEO can spend upwards of a third of her time on them, and leaders throughout the company typically spend 40 percent of their time preparing for them, participating in them, and acting on items that come out of them. Given that they are already a centerpiece of running the business, it makes sense to use them to shift power, change resource allocation, and reshape behavior. Using reviews to their full potential is a skill that can be honed and will improve the return on your scarce time.

Here are guidelines for turning reviews into tools for making the organizational tilt.

Include more people from the South. The mix of people in most reviews does not reflect the new reality of those companies. Leaders from the big-growth areas should be present, because much of the value of reviews is on the social side. The intensity of discussion about business issues forces people to connect socially as well as intellectually. The key is to draw out the people who for cultural or language reasons may hold back, so that the dilemmas and contentious issues between those in the North and in the South come to the surface. Some leaders travel to the various countries to conduct reviews of local leaders, a practice that demonstrates the importance of those people and is a great chance to learn more about the local context.

Use reviews to learn and observe. Reviews are a great opportunity to observe the behavior of individuals and groups. You'll see whether the desired shifts are taking place. Are the people from the North investing enough time in the South to understand local conditions? Are people genuinely aligned on purpose, goals, priorities? When you're tuned in to these things in budget and operating reviews, they're actually pretty easy to detect. You'll also learn a lot about the people. You'll see who the risk takers are—including those who might be taking too much risk—and who's not being bold enough or shifting their priorities and focus. You might find that approvals from North to South are taking too long and discover who is blocking or facilitating. Assuming that the questions and discussions go as deep as they should, reviews are a great help in learning about local conditions and seeing the global picture through another set of eyes.

Turn presentations into dialogue. Many reviews have a common shortcoming: One hour and fifty minutes spent on a PowerPoint presentation, ten minutes reserved for discussion. That has to change. Reviews are most effective in shifting behavior when the group engages in discussion and debate, guided by the leader. Presentations should be limited to maybe fifteen minutes, and items that need discussion should be on a slide up front.

Create linkages. Look for ways to connect the content of one review with that of another. For example, if you learn in an operating review that a leader in the South needs more technical talent, probe the issue with the people who exert influence. Is the head of engineering giving the right people to the South? Is HR allowing enough flexibility in compensation to recruit the right kind of people?

Give feedback. Follow up each review with feedback to the individuals in real time. Your coaching will have a powerful effect on their behavior and their willingness to make often painful shifts in power and resources. Recap the salient points from the discussion and tell them what you liked. Consider what assumptions they should change, and don't hold back on what they can do better. Don't let "blocking" behaviors go unchallenged.

6.

ARE CRITICAL DECISIONS BEING MADE IN THE RIGHT WAY?

You may be clear about the direction and goals of the broader strategy—for example, to get an increased percentage of revenue from the South—but unless you can make good decisions in a timely fashion, the organization will not be able to deliver on them. So you need to rethink what decisions need to be made at headquarters or at the regional or local level and which will require joint decision making or collaboration and negotiation. Isolate your critical decisions and rethink the reasons for making those decisions at headquarters. A typical example is developing a product for the globe, when the country with the highest sales has slowing growth while the competition from low-cost countries is intense. Each of three critical countries is asking for substantial customization. Should the entire development of the product take place in one of those three countries?

A lack of confidence and trust in the local leaders is a separate issue you'll need to address. But assume that you have strong leaders in place. You're likely to see compelling reasons to increase the decision-making power of local people in the South. This is one of the most difficult things for management to change, because people at headquarters feel either that their power is being diminished or risks are too high when they are held accountable for the global consequences of decisions that are highly influenced by leaders in distant places whom they barely know. The litmus test is whether your local leaders can use the power of scale or scope as they make sound decisions as quickly as the toughest local competitor.

A strategy is only as good as the decision makers who operationalize or execute it, and deep knowledge of the local context is crucial. Take, for example, a medical-device manufacturer that was number five in its industry globally and set its sights on the Chinese market. It was late to enter that market. Although the strategist at headquarters had visited the country several times and had ambitious expansion plans, her experience in China was limited, and the company had no local leaders on the spot to guide its thinking. She decided that the best way to catch up would be to sell through distributors. She presented the idea to the board, and—serendipitously, as it turned out—a member was an experienced Chinese businessman. He asked whether it wouldn't be better to build the sales force. While it may be slow and cost more money, he argued, its value is enduring. He explained his reasoning: China is very backward in the usage and servicing of sophisticated medical devices, and the equipment must be demonstrated. Building its own sales force and service team would give the company a long-term competitive advantage. Headquarters agreed and increased the budget to develop sales and service, an approach that is proving to be successful. Without his deep knowledge of the local scene, the company would have missed the reality and its foray into China would have gone bust.

The extent of the local person's authority has to be defined. What approvals does he or she need? There are several areas where local leaders should be empowered:

Hiring and compensation. Local leaders should be able to hire and determine the compensation of key people to fit the local conditions without having to get case-by-case approval from headquarters. The local leader might be given a band or range to operate within, but only after corporate HR has taken time to learn about the conditions. Because of the tight competition and high increases in wages in some places, that band might have to be adjusted more frequently than corporate HR is used to, and there may be some unhappiness that people in the North are not getting the same kinds of salary increases. Nevertheless, when talent is scarce, low salaries and delays in making offers can mean missing out on the best recruits. Headquarters might be concerned that local leaders are giving away the store, but that's where trust in their competence and judgment comes into play. HR should get out and kick the tires—investing time in visiting local operations, learning the local conditions, and getting to know the local leaders. Giving control of hiring and compensation to local leaders shouldn't stop the local people from getting corporate involved, for example, in interviewing job candidates. Developing mutual trust while allowing the local leader to make the final call paves the way to better decisions.

Adapting strategy. Local leaders should have some leeway in tailoring the strategy to their conditions and deciding how to execute it. For example, if the company has three product lines, those leaders should be able to decide which ones to emphasize or expand fastest based on competitive dynamics and what stage of development the local market is in. Such empowerment is problematic to most matrix organizations. There needs to be a consensus about what mix makes more sense in the long term, while allowing local leaders flexibility in day-to-day execution.

Decisions about whether to expand through acquisitions, joint ventures, or greenfield are complicated, but particularly in the area of partnerships and acquisitions, locals need to be able to act in the fast-moving game. It should be clear that they are expected to tap the expertise at headquarters and any consulting firms or investment bankers the company retains, but ultimately they are in the best position to know which targets to pursue. They and headquarters should agree ahead of time on the scale of acquisitions and partnerships that fall within their purview. The legal agreements also should be done collaboratively.

Pricing. Leaders who are close to the ground have the best view of local competitive dynamics and should have the power to deal with them within general guidelines. They may face a low-cost competitor that doesn't compete head-to-head elsewhere, or their local competitors might have a different cost structure. Prices might have to be aggressively lower or higher than elsewhere, at least temporarily, to get a grip on the market or to achieve the same market positioning.

One of the constraining guidelines may be the need to link local pricing decisions with pricing elsewhere. In this transparent world you cannot have major anomalies from one country to another, particularly when customers are themselves multinational. It's not just absolute pricing, it's the structure of pricing—the duration of the terms, the mix of products and services, and other kinds of support, such as financing. These factors might vary, even if price does not.

For some types of decisions, the important shift is in getting information from the South before proceeding. Many products and service offerings are partially standardized and the rest customized to the local market. Technical products are often based on common "platforms." Determining the specifications that will apply across the globe or region is a very tough task that demands balancing inputs from various countries. Often decisions are driven by people in the North who make their judgment calls on a narrow set of needs and price points. The problem is exacerbated if the people in the South aren't practiced in advocating their viewpoint or presenting data. Yet another conflict can arise because the market in the South may be still developing and thus not seem urgent to the Northern manager. Relationships also come into play.

Mechanisms supporting those decisions might have to change. For example, the product-unit leaders might be required to confer more frequently with leaders in the South. As with any social mechanism, frequent contact builds relationships and helps information and ideas flow better. Regardless of who makes the final decision, collaboration will improve the outcome.

Which radical change to tackle first—in organizational structure or in the social system—is a choice leaders have to make. My belief is that driving the tilt in your organization's social system to achieve a better balance between the North and the South will lead you to the right organizational structure. It will likely be unique to your situation. The process of answering the questions this chapter poses will tell you what actions you need to take now, including changing some of your own habits, such as how you conduct reviews.

The changes you decide to make, in whatever sequence, will likely seem doable. Yet they will drive big organizational shifts. As those occur, the next line of action will emerge, and eventually you'll be ready to tackle organizational structure. As you change the content and composition of reviews, for example, you might see that the blockages are occurring because of too many reporting layers or information filters. You may want to eliminate some layers that are filters rather than value creators. You might see that the complexity of having, say, two hundred country managers is bogging down communications and new-product development.

One solution is to reduce the geographic scope. Another could be structural: Organize some countries into clusters or regions and create new means of collaboration using digital tools. You'll get to know your leaders better, and perhaps some who stand out. To retain them and leverage their skills, you might want to elevate them, which again suggests changing or streamlining reporting relationships. In any case, the shifts in power, resources, and behavior will make your company better able to compete in today's tilted world and make changes in organizational structure less ominous.

CHAPTER SEVEN

NORTH COMPANIES AT THE FRONT

MAKING BETS ON MARKET GROWTH

A n outside-in, future-back assessment of growth opportunities almost always points to markets in the
South, but how should you go after them? You don't want
to spread resources too thin (a takeaway from P&G's recent pullback to fewer product markets) or commit them
too soon, nor do you want to compromise your technological edge by sharing it with customers or partners that
may have different goals—or whose governments might.
Since you can't always get what you want in an imperfect
world, realism and pragmatism must rule your decisions
about where to compete, how to compete, and even when
to compete.

Realism comes from the accuracy of your information
and perception. The outside-in, future-back view of the
world does not always yield a pretty picture for leaders in

the North. Sometimes it forces you to accept that competitors have tailwinds you don't have, that the walls between industries are collapsing, or that you're on the road
to losing control of an input you critically rely on. With
courage, you can turn such harsh realities to advantage by
making bold moves.

That's what the leaders of Borealis did. The $9 billion
company headquartered in Vienna, Austria, with extensive
ownership by and operations in the Middle East, is one of
the world's largest makers of polypropylene and polyethylene. Its evolution over the past fifteen years has been
shaped by its reading of two realities: a tilt in the control
of critical inputs and the competitive trend toward vertical integration of the industry. From its roots in a fragmented European petrochemical landscape it has become
a global powerhouse, largely because it took the painful
but necessary steps that ensured its survival in the face of
the growing power of those who controlled the resources
it relied on.

Many well-known consumer-goods companies have
been selling their products in the South for many years—
Nestlé, Unilever, Coca-Cola, and Colgate, for example.
They started early and grew slowly as they built their
brands and distribution networks. Luxury-goods makers
such as Burberry, Prada, and Louis Vuitton waited for a
critical mass of high-end consumers to emerge before es-

tablishing retail outlets for their global brands. But some industrial businesses, those that sell their products and services to other businesses, are taking a different tack to gain enduring competitive advantage in the South. What works for them is a "people first, hard investment second" approach in which they develop local expertise ahead of market growth and thus lay the foundation to expand with the local economy.[1] They identify markets where growth is likely to take off and build the local people engine by hiring a core group of local leaders and technical experts, developing their skills and assimilating them into the company's culture, and building relationships with the local manufacturers that are the future customer base.

A close connection with the customer's technical people gets established early and deepens over time. The trust that develops allows the company to link with the customer's processes and spot new opportunities, which often are high value and high margin. As the economy takes off, the core group of experts scales up; research labs and manufacturing follow, and the company grows along with its industrial customers. Latecomers find it hard to compete against this long-term competitive advantage. 3M and Delphi are among the B2B companies that have committed to markets ahead of growth.

Committing to markets early is not for the shortsighted or the overambitious. It requires long-term investment and, as important, close management attention to the leaders in nascent markets.

Other companies have found partnerships the best way to move forward. North-South partnerships and supplier relationships are staples of the modern business landscape. Many companies from the North—automakers, PC makers, and manufacturers of pharmaceuticals, consumer electronics, high-speed trains, and even industrial glass—have entered into such arrangements in pursuit of the South's lower costs and higher revenue growth. Local partners can provide important competencies required to succeed in those unfamiliar environments, where going it alone can be a minefield or a time drag.

The decision can get complicated in some markets. China, India, and Malaysia, among others, limit the ownership stakes of foreign companies that open shop there in at least some industries. The problem comes when the Northern company is expected to transfer technology and know-how to its partner. For companies whose competitive edge is based on deep expertise and proprietary technology, the prospect of sharing, collaborating, and partnering then becomes a different calculus: Will the partner assimilate the technology and know-how and become a direct competitor? It's a frequent concern in China, which likes to target attractive growth industries, use its market size to entice companies that possess the required expertise, insist that those companies partner with Chinese companies, then use the know-how gained from the joint venture to compete against partners. This has been the pattern in the automobile industry and high-speed trains.

If creating a future competitor is the rock, conceding growth markets to existing competitors is the hard place. Some companies of the North are willing to squeeze into that tough spot, betting that their future will be more—not less—secure if they team up with a player even if it might someday turn against them. Aware of the risks and previous failures, they rely on their ability to choose and manage them to forge ahead. Depending on the market access, technology, and material inputs you need, the relevant question may be not whether to collaborate or forge a dangerous liaison but how to make it work well for you. Companies that succeed can shoulder past the competition. The pragmatists who are willing to cede some control and commit to finding ways to continually differentiate their business are laying claim to the present and perhaps the future. That's the conclusion GE reached when it formed a joint venture with China to tap into Asia's burgeoning aviation market.

Let me describe the dilemma GE faced, the threat Borealis saw, and the groundwork 3M laid as examples of how Northern companies can successfully navigate the tilt and not get beaten by it.

THE LOGIC OF GE'S
CHALLENGING PARTNERSHIP

Some companies from the North enter into partnerships knowing full well that they will be expected to share their technology and know-how and that someday the partner might use those very things to compete against them. What seems like a deal with the devil is really a calculated risk. In some cases, such a partnership is the surest and best way to stay in the game, especially when inaction would relegate the company to low growth and leave it vulnerable to other players that might take the deal. As the partners pool their knowledge, resources, and access to customers, both sides benefit. The risk is that the terms will change at some point in the future—this has happened in the past—or that the partner will allow the expertise to flow to other entities. The decision is always a tough one, also because it gets to be personal. People sense that their jobs are on the line. Slow job growth in the North, combined with Northern companies' emphasis on global expansion, creates a toxic mix of fear and anxiety that stops many leaders in their tracks. The "right" answer for a particular business rests on the finest of judgments about competitive actions and reactions, potential gains and losses, and what the government will do in the future.

Among the most sensitive partnerships of all are those

in industries China has targeted as strategic. A great example of entering such a partnership is GE, which in 2011 formed a fifty-fifty joint venture with Aviation Industry Corporation of China (AVIC), a state-owned enterprise, to jointly bid on avionics, or electronic control systems, for the C919, a narrow-body plane China is developing. The U.S. Defense Department approved the joint venture with AVIC, but the arrangement still raised concerns about whether GE was pursuing its own success at the expense of its home country. A *Wall Street Journal* headline in September 2011 read: "China Venture Is Good for GE But Is It Good for U.S.?"[2] Concerns fell into two camps: Would the deal mean that the United States would lose jobs to China, and would GE lose its competitiveness by giving away cutting-edge technology? But there was another way to look at it: If GE failed to partner with the Chinese, would it concede the market—and lose its relative scale—to non-U.S. competitors, hurting the company and the U.S. economy in the long run? GE's decision to partner with the Chinese represents the hard choices some leaders are making with a clearheaded, outside-in, future-back view of the landscape—and an outcome that is impossible to predict.

The aviation industry is complex, sophisticated, highly interconnected, and beginning to tilt. In 2012 the market for large civilian aircraft (those that carry hundreds of passengers over long distances) is dominated by two companies: Boeing and Airbus. The difficulty and expense of producing large planes and the importance of a safety record raise huge barriers to entry. For regional jets, most of which seat less than one hundred people and fly shorter distances, Brazil's Embraer and Canada's Bombardier are market leaders. Both of these companies grew tremendously with the increase in regional air traffic in the 1990s.

Now with the tilt in economic growth comes an increase in air travel and a concomitant rise in demand for commercial airplanes in the South. Each year since 1964 Boeing has prepared a "current market outlook" in which it projects the demand for large, twin-aisle, and single-aisle airplanes and regional jets over the next twenty years. It makes this information public "to help airlines, suppliers, and the financial community make informed decisions." According to its 2012 report, the number of planes in the world will nearly double by 2030. Deliveries of new planes will total 33,500 over the twenty-year period at a value of $4 trillion. (Airbus does a similar forecast, which for the same time period is only slightly lower.) The United States will be the largest market, mostly to replace existing airplanes, and China will be the second-biggest market. The Asia-Pacific region will need 11,450 new airplanes, valued at $1.5 trillion. The greatest demand for large planes will be from Asia, and the greatest demand overall will be for single-aisle planes because of their cost-efficiency.[3]

Established aircraft manufacturers and their extensive web of suppliers are eager to participate in that growth, but so are some new entrants, namely Russia, Japan, and China, and they are joining the complex web of suppliers and partnerships that characterize the industry, tapping into existing technology and know-how on the way to developing their own.

Big airplanes are enormously complicated machines that integrate hundreds of thousands of parts, from body parts to engines to multiple electronic control systems, all of which must work together. In his book *China Airborne*, James Fallows describes just one challenge, that of cockpit integration: "This would be like designing high-end computer software—for a computer that must simultaneously monitor and control high-temperature power plants; operate and test electrical systems with thousands of connectors and many miles of cable; give pilots the data they need to control a vehicle that can weigh nearly a million pounds and travel at nearly the speed of sound; and do countless other functions, all with triple redundancy or more, and with the constant potential of having to switch to emergency-rescue mode."[4]

Suppliers are numerous and specialized, and often

work closely with other companies to innovate, coordinate, and share costs. Sometimes they form joint ventures; sometimes they outsource to smaller companies. When in the early 2000s Russia began to work on the Superjet 100, a seventy-five- to one-hundred-passenger jet that it hoped would undercut Embraer and Bombardier on price, it got Boeing to collaborate. (Boeing already employed 1,200 Russian engineers at its design center in Moscow.) Parts came from many sources outside Russia: engines from Snecma, electronics from Thales, brakes from Goodrich. An innovative "active aviation system" to warn pilots of emergencies was jointly developed by Russians (the Central Aerohydrodynamic Institute and Sukhoi) and Germans (Liebherr Aerospace), and other parts came from Honeywell, Curtiss-Wright, Parker Hannifin, and Messier-Bugatti-Dowty.

With the launch of the Superjet 100 into commercial service in 2011, a consolidation of Russia's leading aircraft companies under one umbrella called the United Aviation Corporation (UAC), a $10 billion infusion of seed money to UAC, and other regional jets in the works, Russia has made it clear that it's in the aviation game to stay. Japan is also upping its role in aviation. Japanese heavyweights Mitsubishi Heavy Industries, Ishikawajima-Harima, Kawasaki, and Fuji have been suppliers to the aerospace industry for many years. Their parts figured heavily in

Boeing's 777 and 787, particularly in the area of composites, and Japan already produces small jets and turboprop airplanes. Inevitably, the Japanese are moving toward building their own aircraft. Mitsubishi, for example, has been developing its own regional jet, the MRJ (Mitsubishi Regional Jet), with a target date of 2016.

China, of course, has the biggest plans. It is already part of the aviation ecosystem as a low-cost manufacturer and assembler. Now its twelfth five-year plan makes explicit its intent to move up the value chain, and the government has taken the numerous and diverse companies in its aviation industry under its wing to make them more globally competitive. In the early 1990s, that wing was called AVIC, short for Aviation Industry Corporation of China. AVIC later split into AVIC I and AVIC II, each focused on discrete segments of the aerospace industry. In 2007 both became part of state-controlled COMAC (Commercial Aircraft Corporation of China). As in other industries the Chinese government has targeted, its oversight of the entire industry through COMAC has several advantages, not the least of which is government funding with "patient" capital. But COMAC also can control internal competition, use its clout to negotiate on behalf of individual entities, and influence the purchase decisions of the Chinese airlines, which are also state controlled.

The ARJ21, the first-ever Chinese-made regional

jet—albeit much of it subcontracted out to non-Chinese companies such as GE for engines, Rockwell Collins for avionics, and Honeywell for flight-control systems—took its first test flight in 2007. The seventy-eight- to ninety-five-seat regional jet was a direct competitor to Bombardier and Embraer. That same year, Bombardier signed a long-term agreement to work with the Chinese on the next version of the ARJ21, committing its technical support as well as $100 million, making it both a supplier and a competitor.

Then the Chinese went for the jugular, announcing plans to make the C919, a narrow-body plane seating up to two hundred passengers. With the C919 China was stepping squarely into the most popular market space, which Boeing and Airbus dominated. At the June 2011 Paris air show, Jim Albaugh, then head of Boeing's civil jet division, acknowledged the serious changes that were afoot: "The days of the duopoly with Airbus are over," he said.[5] A February 2012 report from Deloitte, "2012 Global Aerospace and Defense Industry Outlook," said of China's ARJ21 and C919: "Together, these two aircraft launch programs represent the emergence of an industry that has struggled over time, but now appears to be emerging as a credible producer of commercial air transportation products."[6] In another twist, Russia's UAC and China's COMAC announced in May 2012 that they would cooperate in building long-haul aircraft.[7]

With the aircraft industry in flux, suppliers have had to figure out what the shifting sands mean for them. Will they grow with the new players—indeed help them grow—or be left out? That's the question GE had to answer in 2011 as it contemplated a joint venture with AVIC to develop and market avionics.

GE has been in the aviation industry for almost a hundred years, having evolved from making turbo-boosters in World War I to being the leading supplier of large commercial and military aircraft engines today. GE Aviation leases airplanes and maintains engines. It got into avionics much more recently. Throughout the years, GE has retained its lead despite sometimes dramatic shifts in technology and markets over the decades. For example, in the early 1990s, it developed engines for regional jets when the pattern of air travel was favoring shorter routes. How GE should proceed and how it would fare in the current reordering was up in the air.

The hard facts were these:

- China will need five thousand new airplanes by 2030, valued at $600 billion, making it the second-largest market.

- The Chinese government is most likely going to influence which planes Chinese airlines buy.
- China has set its sights on exporting the C919 to Southeast Asia, Africa, and South America.
- The Chinese insist that suppliers to the C919 set up joint ventures and transfer their technology.

GE wasn't afraid of partnerships; they were common in aviation and had long been part of GE's vocabulary. In the 1970s it created a joint venture with France's Snecma, which operates as a subsidiary of GE to this day; in 1996 it formed a partnership with its archrival engine maker Pratt & Whitney, and in 2004 it created a joint venture with Honda to create an engine for business jets. Joint ventures in China also were not new to GE; the company already had more than twenty of them across all its businesses. It had supplied engines for China's ARJ21 and had agreed to provide them for the C919 as well through its joint venture with France's Safran Group.

The near-term benefits of partnering with a Chinese company were obvious: GE would eliminate China as a competitor and gain a near-term source of revenue. So were the risks. What would prevent China from assimilating the technology and using it to compete against GE? And what could stop the Chinese government from changing the rules of the game going forward? Avionics is every bit as sophisticated as anything coming out of Silicon Valley, and GE Aviation is among a handful of companies that have worked hard and spent heavily to be at the cutting edge. In 2009, for example, it acquired Naverus, Inc., a company that pioneered a next-generation navigation system called required navigation performance (RNP), which allows more fuel-efficient flight paths and safer landings at airports with challenging terrain and poor visibility by relying on satellite rather than ground control. Within the limitations laid down by the U.S. Department of Defense to safeguard military applications, technology would be shared with the Chinese. So the risk that China would assimilate the technology and compete was unavoidable, as was the risk that the government could change course.

Yet declining to partner with China could marginalize GE in its existing and potential markets and put it at risk of falling behind technologically. And where might it turn to make up the difference in sales? Russia? Russia wasn't close to the scale of China, and it too was anxious to build capability under the watch of a heavy-handed government. Japan's Mitsubishi was building a regional jet and was already in the business of avionics. Bombardier had close ties with China through its joint venture. Would that venture sway other purchasing decisions by Bombardier? There simply were no soft targets. What about the impact in America? Growing U.S. jobs in the near term might force deeper cuts later if GE's aviation business fell behind. Besides all that, such a partnership would give GE Avionics a source of engineering talent and the chance to move up from its number four position. That opportunity is rare, given that any marriage of airframe and avionics is a long-term relationship.

The decision about whether to partner with AVIC ultimately boiled down to how GE would draw the lines around its future market. To frame it as a future-back analysis, the question was this: Should GE go for a larger share of its existing market or a smaller share of a much larger global market? The decision fell to Jeff Immelt, who wasn't keen on fighting for shares of a shrinking pie. He opted instead for the smaller share of a big global market. Rather than being a U.S. company facing a new competitor out of China, GE Aviation would be a global company competing from a base in the South, where the biggest market was. And if the joint venture worked well, it could be a base from which to export to other growth markets.

GE has taken steps to protect its future. One was to insist on at least half ownership of the joint venture, a point that Immelt fought hard for. Another was to commit to staying at the leading edge through ongoing commitment to R&D. The joint venture is chartered to create and protect its own intellectual property, and will focus only on civil applications. Meanwhile, GE will grow its other aviation products and services. While concerns about the loss of proprietary technologies and knowledge are headline grabbers, competitiveness can be maintained in other ways, such as the ongoing ability to innovate and the know-how to link innovation with manufacturing. Technology is never static—others can get ahead of you, and you can get ahead of others. Differentiation comes from a combination of factors—customer service, speed of decision making, and relationship building, as well as innovation. That means having the organizational and people abilities to outrun competitors, regardless of who joins the race, and keeping your DNA of innovation world-class with or without partners.

WHY BOREALIS MERGED WITH THE MIDDLE EAST

Along with opportunities, the tilt exposes threats that, if not attended to, can restrain a company's growth. Borealis saw that its future would be limited because there were not enough attractive opportunities in Europe and because control of its raw materials had essentially shifted to the South. It couldn't plan to grow without dealing with that issue.

Companies of the North dominated the petrochemicals industry from its birth, turning crude oil and natural-gas components—so-called feedstocks—into basic chemicals that could be further processed into products such as paints, plastics, fertilizers, and synthetic fibers. But beginning in the 1990s, as demand for petrochemicals increased, scale, technological capability, and access to attractive feedstock became increasingly important advantages in meeting customers' new and emerging needs while simultaneously succeeding in a globalizing economy. European companies were technologically proficient, but because they were somewhat fragmented, they had no real scale and in addition lacked attractive feedstock opportunities. Restructuring and consolidation began. It was during that time that Borealis, now based in Vienna, Austria, emerged when two Nordic companies combined their petrochemical interest: Neste of Finland and Statoil of Norway. Neste had technology to make polyolefins, and Statoil had access to ethane, a critical raw material, from the North Sea. Still, the combined entity needed greater scale and efficiency to be globally competitive, so it continued to merge, reduce the number of sites, and improve technology. In 1998 Borealis merged with PCD Polymere from Austria's OMV Group to consolidate Borealis's new position as the largest producer of polyolefins in Europe and the fourth largest worldwide. Yet its leaders were prescient to recognize the crucial need to secure access to attractive feedstocks, which were limited in Europe, and they began to search for potential partners throughout the Middle East and Asia.

Other players were also on the move, notably those in the Middle East, where oil and sovereign wealth made a potent combination. Governments wanted to harness the value of their oil and gas and sought various ways of doing so. In 1998, Borealis and the Abu Dhabi National Oil Company (ADNOC) found each other. They formed a joint venture to build an ethane "cracker" (which breaks complex molecules into simpler ones) and two factories to make polyethylene as part of a production complex called Borouge. The matchup gave Borealis the raw material it needed, and Abu Dhabi benefited from technology transfer, job creation, and value addition to its abundant feedstocks. Until that time, if you flew over the Middle East, you'd have seen a lot of flares, where gases that are the by-product of oil drilling were burning off. These gases are now captured, cracked, and then converted into polypropylene or polyethylene, which are solids that can be transported easily. The process solves an environmental problem for Abu Dhabi and secures for Borealis and Borouge a critical input at an attractive price.

Such complex plants require long lead times to build and even longer lead times to run optimally. The Borouge plant went live in 2001, and by 2008 it was producing six hundred thousand tons of polyethylene a year, adding to the 3.5 million tons produced in Europe. In 2005, as plans were laid to build a second facility—Borouge 2—to add 1.5 million tons of capacity, Austria's OMV expanded its ownership stake to 36 percent, while Abu Dhabi's state-owned International Petroleum Investment Company (IPIC) increased to 64 percent. The new ownership arrangement not only ensured that $3.5 billion of "patient" capital would be available to fund Borouge 2, but it also shifted the center of gravity for the former European business to the Middle East. Europe was still outproducing Borealis's Abu Dhabi facilities, but it wouldn't be for long. Borouge 2 came online in 2011, followed by plans for the next project, Borouge 3, to start up in 2014 for a total of 4.5 million tons versus Europe's 3.5 million.

The critical input of ethane gas determined where and to some extent how fast Borealis would grow, even as expansion in Abu Dhabi posed other kinds of challenges. Abu Dhabi is sparsely populated, so building the Borouge plants required many foreign workers. Some twenty-three thousand contractors were on site during the peak building of Borouge 2, requiring complicated logistical support to provide the food, water, housing, and even toilets they needed in the middle of a desert. The projects also required a lot of technical support, which came mostly from Europe, to adapt plant layouts and running conditions to the local environment. In the desert, sandstorms are not uncommon, and outside temperatures can reach 130 degrees Fahrenheit, a far cry from the minus-40-degree temperatures Borealis's plants had to withstand in places like Finland and Norway.

Career tracks also changed for the engineers and production experts, who were mostly European born and educated. They had to face the fact that progressing in the company likely meant living in the Middle East, and they had to be prepared to adapt to the new culture. The company created training programs to help them do so. Mind-sets had to shift as well, to adapt to Abu Dhabi's longer planning time frame. As Borealis CEO Mark Garrett explains: "In Europe, the U.S., and even China, the saying goes that time is money. But in the Middle East, the philosophy is different. They say time is coming to you, not running away from you. That's a crucial difference, especially when you're sitting on 10 percent of the world's oil. It is not in their long-term interest to force their gas fields to overproduce. They believe what is best for them is a steady and consistent development over time. Borealis would never propose things that are not in the best interest of Abu Dhabi. We work together with our owners and our partner ADNOC."

HOW AND WHY 3M COMMITS TO
MARKETS AHEAD OF GROWTH

More than a century old and with revenues of around $30 billion, 3M is known as one of the world's great innovation companies. Its products range from Post-it notes, adhesives, and abrasives to microneedles used for medical purposes and nonwoven filters used for respirators, and it has developed a powerful capability in tailoring its products for local markets. For decades it has expanded into new countries by putting people on the ground, retaining and developing local leaders, and building customer relationships far ahead of market growth. Its investment in research labs and manufacturing facilities follows, based on signals about the emerging needs of the market. For markets that are too small to be self-sustaining, it uses nearby manufacturing hubs. Thailand, for instance, provides products for Indonesia, Malaysia, Vietnam, and the Philippines. As expertise develops in local markets, it creates centers of excellence that seed customer solutions in other markets.

The company began expanding outside the United States in 1950 and has become highly skilled in timing its entry into markets, getting in early enough to build capability and waiting as long as it takes for the market to grow. For example, it put down roots in Indonesia some forty years ago, and for most of the decades since, the Indonesian economy didn't grow. But 3M gradually built its small presence there, bringing local managers and engineers into the corporate fold and selling basic products produced elsewhere to the country's nascent industrial base. Now that the Indonesian economy has begun to take off, 3M's "localization" model has kicked in: The company is modifying products and services for local needs and does R&D and product development for that market, all with predominantly local talent. Jay Ihlenfeld, 3M's head of Asia, Australia, and New Zealand (APAC) until his retirement in 2012, says: "Because we put the basic human resources and knowledge base in place many, many years ago, we can now accelerate our investments in laboratories and local manufacturing facilities. We can operate as a full-service company from the eyes of our local customers."

Waiting forty years for a big payoff is an unusually long time frame even for 3M, but the same basic principles have guided its fast expansion across Asia over the past decade. APAC currently accounts for about a third of company sales—double what it did four years ago—and the plan is to double it again in the next five years, while advanced countries are expected to grow much more slowly. The mother lode of research is still in the United States, but 3M is creating new "centers of excellence" in Asia.

As it develops and taps the capabilities of local people, it is becoming more attuned to the parts of the world that are growing the fastest, and its commitment to building capability ahead of time means it is prepared to act on the opportunities faster and better than its competitors.

Committing to a market means several things at 3M. First, being present in markets that will be strategically important at some point in the future, because they are expected to expand and possibly serve as an export hub, albeit with timing that is uncertain. Second, building customer relationships along with manufacturing and/or research capabilities in those countries so 3M's presence can expand as the local economy grows. Third, building the leadership and technology expertise needed to run those operations as they grow and prosper.

Establishing trust with customers is a chief aim and benefit of being in a market early. Most of 3M's products are technology based; they provide a solution to a problem the customer is wrestling with in its production process or product performance—sometimes one the customer hasn't even recognized. So intimacy with the customer's products and production processes is crucial. For example, by knowing the specific challenges mobile phone makers face in trying to create bright displays while conserving battery power, 3M has used its expertise in optics and adhesives to develop films that make liquid crystal displays easier to view. All of that requires lots of communication and trust between the technologists in the customer shop and at 3M, as well as collaboration inside 3M to tap its extensive intellectual resources. Technical expertise and customer relationships therefore go hand in hand. As Ihlenfeld explains: "Local product development capability has always accelerated growth in that country, provided the market is ripe. That's why it's important to have people who can react to a market need or an opportunity locally. Somebody sitting outside of, say, China who isn't in the middle of it is not going to see that."

PEOPLE FIRST

When Ihlenfeld was first assigned to run APAC in 2006, the rest of Asia was still relying on leaders primarily from the United States who were sent on three- to five-year assignments to run countries and major operations in the region. That's no longer the case. Almost all of the leaders in Asia now are local people 3M has developed, and some have stepped up to take on major senior-level business responsibilities. This depth of knowledge about the local context makes 3M competitive against local players and gives it obvious advantages over other foreign companies that later try to recruit local talent or transfer leaders from other parts of the company. It creates a truly global talent pool, rather than depending on one country to supply all the leadership or expertise.

3M recruits the high-caliber people it needs in time for them to develop their expertise and adapt to 3M's culture in the usual ways, from industry and on campuses, with one exception: The focus for technical areas is on students working on master's degrees or PhDs rather than on undergraduates. Some 25 percent of 3M's R&D leaders in China are PhDs, many of them hired since 2006. But a strong technical background is not enough. A key criterion is the ability to fit into 3M's culture. "It's fairly easy to spot early on the type of person that would be successful in our culture," Ihlenfeld says. "It doesn't matter what culture or country they come from. It's the attitude that matters, the curiosity, creativity, high energy, and ability to operate in a world that's collaborative and not hierarchical. The ability to connect with people—for an Indian engineer to connect with a process engineer in, say, China—is critical. In Europe, Japan, the U.S., and all over Asia, it's always the same."

Headquarters makes decisions about how capital is allocated, but leaders in each country have a great deal of autonomy in making decisions about how that capital is spent. They also decide what products to develop and how to price them. With that comes accountability for business results. That empowerment comes only after ensuring that the local team's capabilities are sufficient to win in the market.

Technical employees in China might spend months or years in a more mature operation like Japan or the United States to enhance their knowledge and also to build collaborative relationships within the company. For example, a Korean technical manager was recently assigned to China for three years, and another to Singapore. Much of the benefit of sending people to other parts of 3M is to foster knowledge transfer and sharing of technology among subject-matter experts. Someone from Vietnam might benefit more from going to China instead of the United States, which is so much more advanced.

Formal training programs, some at the country level, others at the regional and global levels, build leadership and connecting skills not just for general managers but also for those in R&D. For example, in 2011 3M did a session for Chinese leaders in R&D on innovating for all levels of the product pyramid. (The product pyramid is a concept used to capture a hierarchy of market sizes and needs, from a broad base of entry or basic features to mass market to high performance at the top.) Also in 2011 the company ran a regional program on best practice sharing and recruiting for R&D. Groups conduct mini-

conferences regularly to share information, new products, innovations, and even problems they need help on
across the region. All these mechanisms bring connectivity and collaboration to a high level. Managers' training
specifically addresses the issue of culture—what's important about it and how to preserve it. The commitment to
people development is ongoing and in turn makes people
committed to the company.

How long it takes to build capabilities and win credibility from headquarters varies. In the most highly regulated businesses, such as health care or safety and security,
where compliance is a big issue, it takes longer to win
trust. In Japan and Europe it was a gradual process that
happened over the course of decades. In Asia, countries
have been coming into their own at a fast pace over the
past ten years.

TIMING EXPANSION

Creating manufacturing hubs and adapting product platforms until the local market is big enough to support a
largely self-sufficient operation gives 3M great flexibility
in expanding according to market demand. "It doesn't
make sense to be ahead of the market," Ihlenfeld says.
"The point is to be able to move quickly once things begin
to look more and more attractive." This is where firsthand

knowledge of the country and ties with customers pay off. They provide the signals about when to pick up the pace.

Much of 3M's investment now is going toward China and India, with some investment in higher-tech manufacturing in Singapore. "We have had a very small presence in India for many, many years," Ihlenfeld says, "and all of a sudden, things have exploded. We opened a very nice and significant R&D facility in September 2011 to do local product development, and we have a whole pipeline of factory projects for factory expansion. The emergence of major Indian corporations has created a good market opportunity for us."

Investment is also likely to pick up for countries that are in the early stages of growth, such as Vietnam, Indonesia, Thailand, Bangladesh, and even Cambodia, and 3M is watching for signals to emerge. Ihlenfeld explains: "We constantly probe to see what's going on in those places, what changes are occurring in the marketplace that might cause us to increase investment. We have to have a significant migration of industries into those countries to make them attractive. When we start to see that, then we know that there will be significant business opportunities for us in premium-type products and then we can build out the rest of the product line. We're tracking the migration of textiles and pharmaceuticals to Bangladesh and waiting to see if Cambodia reaches a certain threshold. We've been in the Philippines for decades, yet only recently have we seen triggers to growth. Now we're looking at expanding our options there."

3M has been tracking Indonesia for a long time, but only recently has it seen the political stability that caused it to take a closer look at the opportunities. It brought in a team to take a hard look at whether it made sense to expand the leadership and technical team and make hard investments there. A number of structural changes in Vietnam also warranted closer watching, although the conclusion that it would be the next China seemed premature. "We have to consider its relatively weak government policies and the fact that supply chains are still coming out of China," says Ihlenfeld. "So we'll maintain our presence as multinationals shift their supply chains from China to Vietnam and get ready to supply them out of Vietnam."

Many of 3M's customers are themselves multinationals that are building plants in new geographic areas, and they often pull their suppliers with them as they move. That has been true for the pharmaceutical industry in Bangladesh. Close customer relationships, then, are another great source of signals about where and when to scale up, and even where to focus on selling. Customers often make decisions in one country and manufacture products in another for a period of time. When 3M first entered China, for example, it was common for the actual sales to occur somewhere else. Even today, selling to Taiwanese companies but manufacturing in China requires building relationships in both countries. The pattern is common among emerging economies: Build enough of a presence with businesses that are driven by the domestic economy and wait for supply chains to catch up.

Local talent has to be able to deliver to customers' standards, which sometimes requires getting help from other parts of 3M as skills continue to develop. When Samsung recently opened an operation in Vietnam, it was running an A-level operation, and it needed its suppliers to operate at the same level of quality and service it was used to in Korea. The local 3M team was not experienced with such high-level customer demands, but working within 3M's highly networked, collaborative culture, they got help from their Korean counterparts. (Language was not a problem thanks to serendipity: One member of the team in Vietnam was on temporary assignment from Korea.)

TECHNOLOGY PLATFORMS

As 3M enters new countries and plies its technical knowledge to innovate around customers' problems, a critical mass of expertise naturally emerges. That expertise becomes a "center of excellence," a sort of counterpart to a manufacturing hub, where the company's highest-level experts in that market sector are colocated. A center of excellence in Singapore, for example, focuses on innovations for flexible circuits, and one in Japan for electronic connectors and solutions. They become company-wide go-to sources for technical help and generate "product platforms," a basic technology or design that engineers in other countries can adapt and combine for their local customers. 3M's APAC unit has twelve laboratories and more than twenty centers of excellence.

For many years, when customers were mostly U.S. based, product platforms always came out of the United States. But that's changed dramatically. A number of product platforms in the automotive business have come out of Asia, starting with films to replace paint, a technology that was developed in Japan for the domestic automotive industry. Some new structural adhesive platforms in the automotive area (for use in sealing body parts, for example) have emerged from Europe and are now being adopted in other parts of the world.

China recently has become a center of excellence in high-voltage energy transmission. 3M had been tracking the energy industry there since the head of the electrical market division in APAC visited China more than fifty times over a five-year period in the 1990s. He saw that power generation was an emerging opportunity and began the process of building relationships in China and, at the same time, developing local expertise. Such expertise would be especially important in this particular business. 3M had a long history of serving the energy industry in the United States, but it focused on the low-voltage systems—69 kilovolts or lower—that are most common there. China was gearing up its infrastructure to support high voltage, meaning 110 kilovolts and above, because of the long distances between generation sites and cities, and 3M's existing products didn't transfer, since the materials, processes, and skills needed were completely different.

3M recruited Chinese engineers, some of whom spent time in the United States, sent some U.S. experts to China, and invested in special dedicated laboratory equipment for product development and testing. When China began to invest heavily in building its electricity infrastructure, roughly around 2005, 3M was ready to scale up its staff of indigenous engineers. China became the center of excellence.

The company will eventually manufacture there as well, and the country unit will have its own functional heads, so it will be completely integrated.

Apart from the fact that China is the largest market for high voltage, making it the center of excellence ensures a clean break from old ways of doing things—or from what you might call the organizational rules of thumb. It makes it easier for the innovators to avoid preconceived ideas or assumptions about what can and cannot be done and arrive at a completely new platform. Specifically, the Chinese market's demand for low cost drives the search for low-cost solutions. Researchers who have grown up under such constraints find it easier to accept the creative challenge.

Local specifications for both performance standards and cost frequently create the constraints or conditions the engineers at 3M must work against. They force the use of local raw materials, local processes, and local product design and manufacturing. According to Joe Liu, head of R&D for APAC, it is precisely those constraints that cause the actual innovation, provided people have the talent and attitude to deal with those constraints. He says, "That's a key point: when people do innovation here where the markets require lower price points and certain characteristics that can't be matched by the approaches at headquarters, you have the opportunity to do a good job of it by starting with a clean slate." Five years after 3M established its center of excellence in Shanghai, it has a full range of 110-kilovolt products, which are currently manufactured there as well as in other parts of the world. Research is now shifting to super high voltage—greater than 220 kilovolts—which is where the Chinese power industry is headed.

The decentralization of expertise and closeness to customers strengthens 3M against two kinds of competitors: multinational companies and local players. Because it was starting from scratch, 3M was initially at a disadvantage against multinational companies that have been in the high-voltage business for years, such as Tyco International. But its presence in China makes it cost competitive with the big global players and puts it in the center of information at the operational level, to learn what technical specifications are emerging, for example, or who will be making the decisions. Against local players it has a different advantage. There may be cheaper options, but 3M has higher quality and therefore provides better safety, a factor that is often a top priority. In some cases, customers who went with a local player because of cost later came to 3M for help.

Decisions about which research programs to pursue and when to create a totally new platform are made independently of U.S. headquarters. This is a real shift in resource allocation and delegation of decision-making power to the lowest level, where the opportunities matter, possible because of the trust from headquarters. Decisions follow from discussions over several days among a mix of people from marketing, R&D, the supply chain, and business functions across APAC. Expertise about high voltage is shared globally, formally and informally, through technical forums, exchange events, and workshops. In early

2011, for example, people from around the world gathered in Shanghai for a weeklong session on high-voltage products. That knowledge transfer helps jump-start efforts in other countries, such as India, Vietnam, and Indonesia, where the market for high voltage is emerging, and even in some developed countries, such as the UK and Germany, that have shown interest. So building new expertise for new kinds of customers contributes to the company as a whole, and by doing R&D where the price points are lower, 3M is freeing up R&D capabilities at headquarters for the next generation of technology development, especially in market segments, such as biotech and health care, that may not yet be relevant for some parts of the world but where 3M wants to be at the cutting edge.

LEADERS' ROLES

Entering markets early and scaling up as the market grows requires certain uncommon leadership skills. Leaders have to maintain a broad, long-term view—looking outside in, future back—while gauging how to pace the investment and capability building. Ihlenfeld says the leader's role is more like quality assurance than granting approvals: "I want to make sure that our manufacturing organization is building its capabilities, presence, and production in the way it should and at the right pace. I want to make sure the finance organization is doing what it needs to do to support growth in the various countries. I want to see our laboratories building capability and making connections. So I approach things from a macro issue standpoint, looking to see what gaps we have to fill for us to get where we want to be some five years out and championing that on a corporate basis. And then of course you have the operational oversight, which requires focus on the critical elements to ensure we continue to operate efficiently and effectively while at the same time making sure that the strategy gets implemented.

"For me it's about making sure that we're developing the technical experts, leadership, and marketing experts, and getting all those people networked, developed, and growing. So most of my time is really spent on leadership positions and succession planning, working with the countries on that, building the capabilities of the core staff that we have in the area which is very, very skeletal by the way. And then working out any miscommunication or misunderstandings that have to get resolved."

It's hands-on work that requires the ability to see the nuances of each local market and at the same time imagine and foster ways 3M can help. Joe Liu describes his role this way: "I spend some sixty to seventy percent of my time traveling around APAC so I know what's going on in every laboratory, at least with their key programs and key people. In many pharmaceutical companies I know of, the R&D manager spends the vast majority of their time on administrative issues, budgets, and meetings. Here the travel is connecting people, knowing people, knowing what problems they're working on and what they're discovering. The majority of the time is with the researchers and customers.

"When I'm in a country, I spend time in the labs talking with researchers, not sitting in a meeting room, and I join the local team to talk with customers, which is oftentimes a big 'ah-ha.' In summer 2011 when I visited India, for example, I joined the local health care team to visit the kind of hospitals most Indian people go to for treatment, and that was a big eye-opener. The doctor actually took us to the patient room, opened the covers, and allowed us to see the wounds on the patient. In my whole life I had never seen so many wounds. These are low-income people who cannot afford many of our products. That one visit convinced me that we needed to set price-point constraints that were suitable for that market. How could we combine our mature technology with local raw materials and local process thinking to come up with a product people could afford? And when we do that, it will be applicable to a lot of other countries as well.

"My view is that every market is a growth market. It's just that the challenges are different. We have a large and capable laboratory in Japan, so I pay attention to that, as well as Australia and New Zealand. Then there are places like Indonesia and Vietnam where the GDP is growing at a faster pace, so that can't be ignored. We know from our history that it's the things we do today that set a strong base for R&D and are going to pay off later in a big way."

YOUR GLOBAL FUTURE

As I make the final edits to this book, I continue to hear a constant concern among leaders: How can we grow the business when Japan and Europe are stagnant and the United States is only slowly recuperating? We have to stay competitive in those markets, yet be cost competitive in the growth markets of Asia, South America, and Africa. It seems an impossibility.

But it isn't. Stepping back and taking a broader, longer-term view of the global landscape is the starting place to find big opportunities. That doesn't mean you should abandon incremental expansion of existing markets. Singles and doubles still add up. The real challenge is striking a balance by choice, not by default. That means building your mental capacity to see the big picture and to understand the specifics of various opportunities in the South without losing sight of the business fundamentals. You won't succeed without expanding your knowledge base and adjusting your frame of reference—often. As you think and act differently, your organization will begin to change. That's leadership.

What should a global company look like in the tilt?

- It might have a central headquarters in the South. Or it might have several headquarters—one for each business unit—in various parts of the world. Or it might have no single location with a sizable staff, convening telephonically and rotating face-to-face meetings throughout countries where the company operates.

- It has leaders who keep a keen eye on the macro landscape, form a point of view about it, and find opportunities in it based on information gathered at the ground level—information that does not get homogenized or sanitized on its way through organizational layers.

- It has goals, performance targets, and accountability that are linked to the challenges leaders are facing in real time.

- It redirects resources quickly when a market softens, another begins to take off, or the competition heats up.

- Its decision makers are closely connected to one

another despite physical distance and stay close to the sources of information their decisions rest on.

- It moves decisively ahead of others because leaders are confident in their perception yet vigilant in reading signals that they need to change course.
- It has the psychology to accept that some things are unknowable, and the confidence, flexibility, and resilience to adapt.

This is not an unachievable ideal. It is your future. How can you deny the world's unstoppable trends and the inevitability of economic growth in the South? The more you learn about the South, the more you'll appreciate that you have to operate differently to succeed there. You'll see that it's downright silly to determine a pecking order based on physical distance from a headquarters based in the North, or to skip through a country that represents a major part of your company's growth.

The faster you dissolve the systems, structures, and beliefs that are holding you back, the sooner you'll find that despite the ongoing uncertainty, the world is less ominous than you think. A tilt in the balance of the world's economic power is not the end of the world, nor is a tilt in your leadership and organization. The pace and timing of the global tilt may be uncertain, but the direction is clear.

Adjusting to it will allow you to be part of it, and help you adapt to its inevitable fits and starts.

Remember the universals: the basics of money making, and of people's desire to improve life for themselves and their children. During the global financial crisis, anxiety was widespread, proving yet again that the world is interconnected. People everywhere worried what it would mean for them: Could they pay their mortgage or put food on the table? Businesses pulled back. Some still haven't shaken their defensive stance.

One company adapted quickly to the shock precisely because its modus operandi had already tilted, with a headquarters that was more virtual than real and a diverse team of leaders who had learned to bring current issues to the fore and solve problems jointly—and fast—based on their unfiltered ground intelligence. Even a ban on travel imposed because of cost constraints didn't keep the leaders from bridging the thousands of miles and huge cultural gaps that separated them. AZ Electronic Materials, a supplier to semiconductor and other electronics manufacturers, had operations on three continents in 2008. Just a couple of years earlier, the company had gone through a major shift in how it operated. Its top leaders met face-to-face every other month in places as far-flung as Ridgefield, Connecticut, and Munich, Germany. They met telephonically the alternating months. Their nationalities and native languages differed, so they spoke English at those meetings, some with heavy accents. The focus was always on the big picture of the external environment, the company as a whole, and customers. Competition was cutthroat, customer needs were changing very fast, and margins were thin, so every bit of obsolescence mattered. They pooled their observations to decide which technology to develop, how much and where to produce, and at what price. Goal setting and resource allocation were done among the group.

When the global financial crisis hit, the company had to abruptly shift from trying to expand fast enough to keep up with exploding demand to cutting costs fast enough to stay in the black as that demand collapsed. "All of a sudden business came to a screeching halt," then-CEO Thomas von Krannichfeldt explains. "The party was over and we had to react immediately." They were able to, largely because of the mechanisms they had in place to knit people together and coordinate their thinking and actions. To pare expenses, they suspended the face-to-face meetings, but phone meetings provided the venue to sort things out.

It had been part of AZ's strategy to use multiple sourcing points, but when much lower demand and changes in exchange rates made it more costly to produce in Japan, they had to rethink that approach. Suppliers in Japan were suddenly too expensive to source from. Cutting off those sources, which meant that some production facilities would have to be closed while others were expanding, was a difficult reality to face. Von Krannichfeldt explains:

Rather than sourcing 50/50 or 60/40 from Japan and Europe, the numbers were telling us that 0 percent from Japan and 100 percent from Europe was the smart thing to do. If we didn't make that shift, our competitors might gain a cost advantage. But of course making such a shift is easier said than done. We didn't want to simply force it. It was important to get the key country managers to understand why some were gaining and some were losing.

We had weekly teleconferences with the country managers, supply chain managers and purchasing managers. And despite the fact that it was a fairly large group on the phone, we tried to be as open as possible. We went through the reviews and tried to connect everybody so they could see beyond their parochial approaches. The Japanese had to accept that the yen had strengthened enormously. It had gone down from something like 115 to the dollar to almost 90 at some point. These were huge swings, and there was nothing our suppliers in Japan could do to compete with, say, a German manufacturer or a Korean manufacturer.

This was quite painful, but people came around to accept that perhaps they could no longer source locally, because yes, the numbers speak for themselves. It's too expensive. It costs us a million or two dollars more for a given product if we keep doing this. It makes no sense.

Every company needs flexibility and responsiveness to keep attuned to changing conditions and new opportunities—and to stay financially afloat in the event of a tidal wave that washes in from some unknown corner. I hope this book has convinced you that it is possible to lead confidently in the tilt. In fact, it is your obligation. I urge you to prepare yourself to meet it by developing the mind-set and skills you will need to be a leader in the global tilt.

YOUR GLOBAL LEADERSHIP CHALLENGE IN A
NUTSHELL

Leadership now takes more than the basics. Business acumen, good judgment on people, high integrity and values, the discipline of execution—these and other familiar qualifications continue to be important. But there are new essential skills and abilities you'll need to be a successful leader in the global tilt:

1. Incisiveness to cut through the complexity of the changing global landscape, to spot the unstoppable trends and hinge events, and willingness to devote the time to this activity to keep pace with the speed of change.

2. Imagination to see opportunities before they are fully formed and courage to act in the face of uncertainty, to make the occasional strategic bet based partly on qualitative and sometimes incomplete knowledge.

3. Keen perceptual skills to quickly absorb multiple cultures, understand the rules of thumb in new contexts, and drill through cultural differences to the business fundamentals.

4. Expertise in building social networks and bridges of information with governments, regulators, and other external constituencies.

5. Savvy in shaping and reshaping the company's social system to reduce information filters, speed decision making, establish behavioral norms, and get inherent tensions between headquarters or other centralized units, business functions, and geographies resolved quickly.

6. The breadth and depth of perspective and the cognitive ability to see the big picture, link it to information at the ground level, and shine a light on a path to growth and profitability that energizes others.

7. Discipline to manage your time, keep learning, and do what needs to be done.

ACKNOWLEDGMENTS

This book is the product of my observations of and discussions with some of the world's most successful business leaders—people who are not just surviving today's dizzying speed of change but thriving in it, and in some cases, helping to create the global geo-economic tilt. I am deeply grateful for the time and attention they gave me. Their intellectual engagement stimulated my thinking, and their exemplary leadership is the source of many of the lessons presented in these pages. In particular, I wish to thank Jay Ihlenfeld (retired), Cindy Johnson, Joe Liu, and Inge Thulin of 3M; Kumar Mangalam Birla and Santrupt Misra of Aditya Birla Group; Tom von Krannichfeldt (retired) of AZ Electronics; Sunil Mittal and Manoj Kohli of Bharti Airtel; Mark Garrett of Borealis; Steve Bolze, John Chiminski, John Flannery, Jeff Immelt, and John Rice of GE; and G. M. Rao and Kiran Kumar Grandhi of GMR Group.

I also wish to thank the following highly accomplished business leaders for generously sharing their thoughts and insights: Tripp Ahern, Bob Beckler, Todd Bradley, Dick Brown, Greg Brown, Mike Campbell, Dennis Carey,

Bill Conaty, Mohamed El-Erian, Brad Feldmann, Ken Frazier, Gordon Fyfe, Erik Fyrwald, Manoj Gaur, Chad Holliday, Muhtar Kent, John Koster, John Krenicki, A. G. Lafley, John Luke, Stephanie Mehta, Jac Nasser, John Needham, Rod O'Neal, Tony Palmer, Maria Luisa Ferré Rangel, Hellene Runtagh, Ivan Seidenberg, Deven Sharma, Aniljit Singh, and Mirian Graddick Wier.

John Mahaney, my editor at Crown, applied his unsurpassed expertise in ensuring the best possible experience for readers. John is meticulous in his drive for clarity and specificity. He dedicated an enormous amount of mental energy, not to mention time, to bring this book to fruition. I thank him for his intellectual and editorial contributions, served up with a terrific sense of humor.

Geri Willigan made indispensable substantive and editorial contributions to this book. She applied her usual keen conceptual and analytic mind to a tremendous amount of information. For the past twenty years, Geri has helped me enormously as content developer, writer, editor, researcher, and project manager.

Charlie Burck, a former executive editor at *Fortune* who worked with Larry Bossidy and me on *Execution,* lent his probing intellect and superb writing skills to this project. He has the rare capability to dig deep into a complex subject and communicate it in a way that is easy to grasp.

Researching this book involved dozens if not hundreds of trips to far-flung parts of the world. Cynthia Burr and Carol Davis are the magicians in my Dallas office who kept me moving and on track. Far more than travel agents, they are the infrastructure that allows me to traverse the globe and still function on a daily basis. I am very grateful for their value-added.

I also want to thank the three fine journalists—Geoff Colvin, David Whitford, and Larry Yu—who gave me helpful feedback, as did Jon Galli and my long-time business associate John Joyce. Last but not least, thanks to Mary Choteborsky, Derek Reed, and the rest of the team at Crown for their help, patience, and attention to detail.

And to you, the reader: I am grateful for your desire to learn and improve. It is people like you who will make a better world.

NOTES

CHAPTER 1

1. World Trade Organization, International Trade Statistics, 2012.

CHAPTER 2

1. Charles Roxburgh, Susan Lund, and John Piotrowski, *McKinsey Global Institute: Mapping Global Capital Markets 2011* (McKinsey & Company).

2. Mary Anastasia O'Grady, "Ben Bernanke, Currency Manipulator," *Wall Street Journal,* October 30, 2012.

3. Robin Harding, "IMF Gives Ground on Capital Controls," *Financial Times,* April 5, 2011.

4. Charles H. Ferguson, *Predator Nation* (New York: Crown Business, 2012), p. 223.

5. Ibid., p. 20.

6. Ian Bremmer, *The End of the Free Market* (New York: Penguin Group, 2010).

7. Kenneth G. Lieberthal, *Managing the China Challenge* (Washington, D.C.: Brookings Institution, 2011).

8. Bloomberg News, "Copper: China's Red Gold," *Bloomberg Businessweek* (available at http://www.businessweek.com/magazine/copper-china-redgold/), accessed August 17, 2012.

9. Bill Powell, "Why China Is Losing the Solar Wars," *Fortune,* August 2, 2012.

10. http://www.hbs.edu/competitiveness/

11. James Manyika, Michael Chui, Brad Brown, Jacques Bughin, Richard Dobbs, Charles Roxburgh, and Angela Hung Byers, "Big Data: The Next Frontier for Innovation, Competition, and Productivity," *McKinsey Quarterly,* May 2011.

12. Ibid.

13. Erik Brynjolfsson and Andrew McAfee, *Race Against the Machine* (Lexington, MA: Digital Frontier Press).

14. Karim Sabbagh, Roman Friedrich, Bahjat El-Darwiche, and Milind Singh, "Maximizing the Impact of Digitization," Booz & Co. Inc, 2012.

15. Scott D. Anthony, *The Little Black Book of Innovation* (Cambridge, MA: Harvard Business Review Press, 2012).

16. Anthony, "The New Corporate Garage," *Harvard Business Review,* September 2012.

17. Homi Kharas and Geoffrey Gertz, "The New Global Middle Class: A Cross-Over from West to East," http://www.brookings .edu/~/media/research/files/papers/2010/3/china%20middle%20 class%20kharas/03_china_middle_class_kharas.pdf.

18. Rukmini Shrinivasan, "Middle Class: Who Are They?," *Economic Times* of India, December 1, 2012.

19. Homi Kharas and Geoffrey Gertz, Brookings Institution, in a 2011 report by *Economist,* July 23, 2011.

20. Yougesh Khatri, Wilianto Ie, and Alastair Newton, "Indonesia: Building Momentum," Nomura, June 9, 2011.

21. Matt Moffett, "A Rags-to-Riches Career Highlights Latin Resurgence," *Wall Street Journal,* November 15, 2011.

22. Nouriel Roubini, "Young, Poor, and Jobless," *Slate*, March 8, 2011.

23. Joe Leahy and James Fontanella-Khan, "India: Squeezed Out," *Financial Times*, December 17, 2010.

24. "Steelmakers Accuse Iron Ore Producers of 'Illicit' Price Change," *Financial Times*, April 1, 2010.

25. Press release, March 2010, from the European Automobile Manufacturers' Association, whose members are BMW Group, DAF Trucks, Daimler, FIAT Group, Ford of Europe, General Motors Europe, Jaguar Land Rover, MAN Nutzfahrzeuge, Porsche, PSA Peugeot Citroën, Renault, Scania, Toyota Motor Europe, Volkswagen, and Volvo.

26. Craig Trudell and Mark Clothier, "Auto Output Threatened by Resin Shortage After Explosion," Bloomberg, April 17, 2012.

27. Sanjeev Choudhary, "Indonesia Tax Plan May Turn India Power Firms to Australia, Africa," Reuters, April 4, 2012.

28. James Wellstead, "Indonesia's Coal Game," *Coal Investing News*, April 16, 2012.

29. Choudhary, "Indonesia Tax Plan."

30. Sarita C. Singh and Devina Sengupta, "Foreign Firms Like Rio Tinto, BHP Lure Mining Engineers with Fancy Packages and Perks," *Economic Times* of India, May 15, 2012.

31. Richard Dobbs, Susan Lund, Charles Roxburgh, et al., "Farewell to Cheap Capital?: The Implications of Long-Term Shifts in Global Investment and Saving," McKinsey Global Institute, December 2010.

32. Ferguson, *Predator Nation*, p. 20.

33. Matthew Ruben, "Forgive Us Our Trespasses?: The Rise of

Consumer Debt in Modern America," ProQuest Discovery Guides, February 2009, www.csa.com/discoveryguides/debt/review.pdf.

CHAPTER 3

1. Unless otherwise noted, quotes in this and other chapters are based on my personal interviews.

2. Carlos Brito, interview by Big Think, September 9, 2010, video at http://bigthink.com/users/carlosbrito.

3. Please note that for this discussion of Haier, I drew heavily on facts and quotes from the following two cases prepared by Harvard Business School, which proved to be excellent source documents: Tarun Khanna, Krishna Palepu, and Phillip Andres, "Haier: Taking a Chinese Company Global in 2011," Harvard Business School, August 11, 2011; Krishna Palepu, Tarun Khanna, and Ingrid Vargas, "Haier: Taking a Chinese Company Global," Harvard Business School, August 25, 2006.

4. Patti Waldmeir, "Haier Seeks to Boost European Sales," *Financial Times,* June 18, 2012.

5. Geoff Colvin, "Zhang Ruimin: Management's Next Icon," *Fortune,* July 15, 2011.

6. Sunil Bharti, interview, "Bharti Group's Sunil Bharti Mittal on Lessons of Entrepreneurship and Leadership," *India Knowledge@ Wharton,* July 10, 2008.

7. Ibid.

8. Ibid.

9. Joji Thomas Philip, "We Didn't Imagine 100 mn in Our Dreams: Sunil Mittal," *Economic Times,* May 16, 2009.

CHAPTER 4

1. "Kodak's New Focus," *BusinessWeek*, February 12, 1995, http://www.businessweek.com/stories/1995-02-12/kodaks-new-focus.
2. Andrew Hill, "Snapshot of a Humbled Giant," *Financial Times*, April 2, 2012.

CHAPTER 7

1. Some consumer-goods companies have also put people first. KFC, for example, took care to build a critical mass of managers who could train the many inexperienced workers its restaurants would need before undertaking major expansion in China.
2. John Bussey, "China Venture Is Good for GE but Is It Good for U.S.?" *Wall Street Journal*, September 30, 2011.
3. Boeing, "Current Market Outlook 2012–2031, http://www.boeing.com/commercial/cmo/pdf/Boeing_Current_Market_Outlook_2012.pdf.
4. James Fallows, *China Airborne* (New York: Pantheon, 2012).
5. Mark Odell, "Boeing and Airbus Call Time on Duopoly," *Financial Times,* June 20, 2011.
6. Deloitte, "2012 Global Aerospace and Defense Industry Outlook: A Tale of Two Industries," Deloitte Global Services Limited, February 2012.
7. Yuliya Fedorinova, "Russia, China to Produce New Long-Haul Aircraft, Vedomosti Says," Bloomberg.com, May 30, 2012, http://www.bloomberg.com/news/2012-05-31/russia-china-to-produce-new-long-haul-aircraft-vedomosti-says.html.

INDEX

AB InBev, 120–24
Abu Dhabi National Oil Company
    (ADNOC), 80, 273–76
Accenture, 10, 178
Aditya Birla Group, 114, 117, 180
aerospace, 169, 265
Africa, 5, 70, 72, 181, 200, 268
    Bharti Airtel and, 3–4, 86, 132, 141–
        48, 174, 188–89, 210–12, 223–24
    China preferred as business partner
        by, 11
    Chinese workers in, 76
    communications in, 62–63
    growth in, 88, 295
    Indian business with, 17
Agnelli, Roger, 46–47
AIG, 38–39, 95
Airbus, 262–63, 266
Alcan, 114, 116, 117
Allied Signal, 143, 169
aluminum, 79, 80, 114–20
Amazon, 60, 63, 66, 176
AmBev, 122–23
Andreessen, Marc, 65–66
Anheuser-Busch, 120–24
Anthony, Scott D., 66–67
Apple, 60, 157, 174
appliances, large, 124–31
Arab Spring, 61, 73
arbitrage, 30, 52, 178
Arcelor Mittal, 80–81, 98
Argentina, 121, 168
Asia, 5, 29, 68–69, 82, 88, 119, 200,
    277, 279, 282, 295
Asian Contagion, of 1997, 7, 31
asset price bubbles, 31, 32
AT&T, 86, 174
Australia, 81, 82, 106, 277, 293
Austria, 256, 272, 273, 274
automobiles, 44, 84, 169, 286
    Chinese production of, 15, 161, 259
    driverless, 63
    European production of, 78
    luxury, 100–101

North-South partnerships for, 258
aviation, 8, 14, 35, 178
    GE-China partnership in, 259–71
Aviation Industry Corporation of China
    (AVIC), 261, 265–71
avionics, 261, 266, 269
AZ Electronic Materials, 298–300

Bangladesh, 4, 17, 52, 82, 141, 142,
    283, 284
banks, 29, 34, 86, 142
    global, 10
    regulation of, 93
Bezos, Jeff, 66
Bharti Airtel, 3–4, 34, 70, 86, 98, 132–
    48, 174, 188–89, 210–12, 223–24
Bhattacharya, Debu, 116, 119, 180
BHP Billiton, 77–78
Bihar, 138–39, 143
Birla, Aditya Vikram, 9, 115
Birla, Kumar Mangalam, 98, 108–10,
    112–13, 114–15, 118–20
Boeing, 226, 262, 264, 266
Bombardier, 262, 264, 266, 269–70
Borealis, 80, 256, 260, 271–76
Borouge, 273–75
Bossidy, Larry, 143, 169
Brazil, 5, 11, 14–15, 33, 42, 46–47, 73,
    82, 88, 97, 121, 178, 207, 224, 262
    AB InBev in, 120–24
    national economic strategies in, 7, 32
Bremmer, Ian, 45, 47
Brito, Carlos, 121–24
budgets, 222, 223, 231–35
Buffett, Warren, 94
Busch family, 120, 123

Caceres, David, 72
Cambodia, 83, 283–84
Canada, 52, 86, 114, 117, 121, 170, 262
capital:
    allocation of, 205
    demand for, 88
    excess, 35, 44

capital *(cont.)*
 mobility of, 28–33
 patient, 36–37, 53
 South and, 9
 two-way flow of, 34
capital flows:
 cross-border, 28
 free, 32
capital gains, 32
capital investment, 60
capitalism, 21, 83, 131
 democracy and, 49
 state, 45–49
Caterpillar, 89, 192
centers of excellence, 278, 286–89
CEOs, 201–6
China, 5, 11–12, 46, 58, 70, 72, 97, 119, 121, 181, 207, 208, 275, 280, 313*n*
 aircraft manufacturing in, 8, 178, 259–71
 auto manufacturing in, 15, 178
 Brazilian iron ore in, 14–15
 currency of, 19, 30, 35, 48, 52
 domestic consumption in, 19
 during European Renaissance, 22
 five-year plans in, 49–52
 foreign investments by, 34, 35, 92
 foreign investments in, 8, 29, 30, 33
 GDP of, 47, 51, 54
 GE's partnership with, 259–71
 Haier Group in, 124–31
 as India's largest trading partner, 82
 industries targeted by, 53, 160, 178, 182
 inter-party democracy in, 54
 Kodak in, 156–57
 late entry to, 248–49
 local control in, 50–51
 low labor costs in, 19, 30, 52, 85
 market size of, 30, 203, 259, 263, 268, 287
 middle class in, 69, 74
 national economic strategy in, 7, 31
 Northern partnerships with, 258–59
 opportunities created by, 160–61
 ownership restrictions in, 8, 258–59
 private enterprise in, 54
 quotas and tariffs in, 76–77
 socialist market economy in, 22, 45
 Southern growth of, 16–17
 sovereign wealth of, 29, 35
 state capitalism in, 47–49, 56
 state-owned enterprises (SOEs) in, 36, 51–54
 sustainability of model of, 52–55

 3M in, 280, 281, 283–85, 286–89
 trade surplus of, 19, 21, 29–30, 35, 52
 United States' deficit with, 22, 29, 35, 38, 87
 unreliable information from, 43
 U.S. investment in, 89, 202–3
 water supplies in, 82
coal, 70, 79–80, 236
Coca-Cola, 69, 256
Colgate, 15, 69, 256
collateralized debt obligations (CDOs), 93–95
Colvin, Geoffrey, 131
Commercial Aircraft Corporation of China (COMAC), 8, 265–67
commoditization, 59
commodity prices, 236
communications, 206, 214
compensation, 81–82, 249–50
consumer goods, 60, 313
consumers, 153, 212–13
core competencies, 155–56, 202
 extension of, 161–62
credit default swaps, 94–95
credit flow, 30
currency, 31, 89, 236
 appreciation of, 88, 300
 China's, 19, 30, 35, 48, 52
 dollars, 44–45

dark pools, 41
debt-to-net-capital ratio, 93
decision-making, 215, 223, 247–54
Delhi, 104, 105, 110, 111, 136, 137, 138, 147, 191, 193
Delphi, 160–61, 257
democracy, 56, 57
 capitalism and, 49
 central planning vs., 12
 in China, 54
 in global marketplace, 47
 market protections in, 46
 U.S. push for, 11
Deng Xiaoping, 22
digital photography, 157–58
digitization, 26, 31, 58–65, 83
Donaldson, Bill, 94
Dow Chemical, 163–68

economic ecosystem:
 shift from North to South, 4–5, 10–11
 of South, 16–17, 19
economy:
 China's socialist market, 22

cooling of global, 13
large-scale in, 14
market-based, 54
perfect storm in global, 54–55
real, 28, 87
seismic shifts in, 21–22
slowing global, 3
education, 20, 55, 56, 73–74
electricity, 79
high-voltage, 286–89
electronics, 298
consumer, 127, 128, 258
Embraer, 262, 264, 266
emerging markets, as misleading
category, 17
employment, 73
competition for, 7, 21, 83
exports and, 71
U.S., 260, 270
energy, 51–52, 106, 286–89
entrepreneurs, large-scale, *see* large-scale
entrepreneurs
equality, narrowing gap and, 6, 20–22,
83
equity market capitalization, 28
Ericsson, 140, 141, 146
Essar, 136, 138, 139
ethane, 272, 273
Europe, 3, 30, 35, 54, 71, 77, 127, 135,
174, 192, 200, 208, 230, 271, 275,
282, 300
Eastern, 127
economic shift from, 4–5
financial crisis in, 11, 86, 295
middle class in, 69
Southern investments by, 29
exports, limits on, 76–77

Facebook, 61, 66
Fallows, James, 263–64
Federal Reserve, 32, 39–40, 91
Ferguson, Charles H., 41
Fields, Mark, 215–16
financial crisis of 2008, 28, 37–41, 57,
91–96, 165, 298–99
financial ratings agencies, 40–41, 94,
166, 167, 192
financial services industry, U.S., 36–
37
Finland, 272, 275
Fisher, George, 156–58
Fitch, 40, 94
Flores, Aquilino, 71
Ford Motor Company, 100–101, 119,
243

foreign direct investment (FDI), 31,
34–35, 57
foreign institutional investment (FII),
31, 34–35, 88
France, 69, 117, 135–36, 268
free market, 21
in North, 7, 8, 9–10
in United States, 45, 55, 93
future advantage, 168
"future back" thinking, 161–62
Fyrwald, Erik, 182

Gap, 34, 69, 170
Garrett, Mark, 275
Gates, Bill, 4
GDP, 73, 293
China's, 47, 51, 54
global, 154
General Electric (GE), 10, 20, 27, 127,
181–82, 204, 225, 227–30, 242
Chinese partnership of, 259–71
shift away from plastics by, 158–59
Germany, 14, 21, 53, 69, 125, 128, 179,
230, 264, 290, 300
Gertz, Geoffrey, 67–69
global financial system, 19–20, 26,
28–44, 84
governance of, 39–40
growth of, 28–29
instability of, 6–7, 28, 31–33, 37–42,
86–88
real economy and, 87
global integrators, 213–14
global leadership, 185–87, 207, 301–3
basics of, 189–90
CEOs in, 201–6
challenging rules of thumb in,
212–13
length of postings among, 224–31
moving from North to South, 191–97
for a worldwide business, 197–201
global tilt:
boards of directors and, 203–4
definition of, vii
mobilizing to reality of, 183
models for global companies in,
296–97
new business environment created
by, 25–27
playing by different rules in, 8–9, 26
GMR Group, 102–13
Goldman Sachs, 39–40, 41–42, 93
Google, 60, 63
Greece, credit crisis in, 30
Greenspan, Alan, 39, 91, 93

growth, 26, 153
  cyclical slowdowns in, 11–12
  discrepancies in, 83
  loss in (2007–2012), 7
  in North, 9, 11, 12
  resource allocation and, 15–16
  in South, 12
Gujarat, 98, 138, 142

Haier Group, 52, 124–31
Hamel, Gary, 155–56
Harrington, Dick, 170
herd effect, 87
highway construction, 107–8
Hindalco, 113–20, 180
Hoffecker, John, 79
Honeywell, 20, 143, 169, 227, 264, 266
Hong Kong, 22, 30, 32, 110, 225, 228
Huawei Technologies, 52, 146, 179
Hu Jintao, 54
Hyderabad, 105, 108–10

IBM, 10, 64, 139, 141, 146, 176, 178,
  179
Ihlenfeld, Jay, 277, 279–80, 283–84,
  290–91
Immelt, Jeff, 27, 159, 204, 242, 270
income, inequality of, 74–75
India, 5, 12, 35, 44–45, 97, 180–81,
  182, 192, 200, 207, 208, 236, 187
  age of population in, 72
  business tradition in, 98–99
  coal resources and, 79–81
  communications in, 3–4, 62–63
  currency in, 88
  economic liberalization in, 134–35
  engineers in, 73–74, 81–82, 106, 115
  during European Renaissance, 22
  foreign investment in, 9, 29, 33, 34
  frugal innovation in, 75
  GDP of, 73
  Golden Quadrilateral project in, 105
  Hindalco Industries in, 113–20
  middle class in, 69, 70
  multiple economies in, 70
  national economic strategies in, 7, 31
  outsourcing in, 10, 134, 178
  ownership restrictions in, 8–9
  pharmaceuticals in, 86, 178
  Southern growth of, 17
  3M in, 283, 290, 292
  trade deficit of, 82
  transportation infrastructure in,
    104–5
  wages in, 81–82

water supplies in, 82
Indonesia, 5, 70, 79, 81, 82, 102, 127,
  207, 224, 276
  Northern investments in, 33
  3M in, 277, 283, 284, 290, 293
information, 301
  blockages in flow of, 222, 238–44
  content and architecture of, 206
  inaccurate, 43
information services, 170–71
information technology (IT), 81, 140,
  146, 147
infrastructure, 20, 57
innovation, 56, 59, 65–67
interest rates, 31, 32, 91, 236
International Monetary Fund (IMF),
  31, 32–33
Internet-based marketing, 60–61
iron ore, 77–78, 81
Italy, 47, 230

Japan, 5, 14, 30, 31, 34, 47, 53, 62, 70,
  71, 77, 85, 86, 119, 128, 133, 135,
  208, 215–16, 299–300
  aviation in, 263, 265, 269
  during European Renaissance, 22
  3M in, 281, 282, 286, 293
  trade deficit of, 21
  zero growth in, 54, 295
Jemal, Michael, 128–29
Jobs, Steve, 4, 65

Kashkari, Neel, 40
KFC, 69, 181–82, 192, 231
Kharas, Homi, 67–69
Kodak, 156–58
Kohli, Manoj, 141–48, 188–89,
  210–11, 224
Korea, 127, 135, 281, 285, 300
  North, 46
  South, 5, 22, 53
KPIs, 206, 221, 222, 231, 236, 240
Krannichfeldt, Thomas von, 299–300
Krenicki, John, 159
Kuwait, 29, 132, 164–66

large-scale entrepreneurs (LSEs), 99–
  100, 102–3
Larkin, Leo J., 167
leadership:
  global, see global leadership
  in global tilt, 296–97
  multicontextual, 185–87
  in North, 232
  in South, 233

3M and early market entry, 290–93
Lehman Brothers, 93, 95
Lemann, Jorge Paulo, 122
leverage, 38, 80, 93, 95
License Raj, 105, 134
Lieberthal, Kenneth G., 50–51
Liebherr Aerospace, 125, 264
liquidity, 87, 91, 96
Liu, Joe, 288, 292–93
Liveris, Andrew, 163–67
local context, 198–200, 207–10,
    248–53
long-term economic value, 172–77
Ludhiana, 132–33
luxury goods, 182, 256–57

McAfee, Andrew, 63
McDonald, Bob, 242–43
McKinsey Global Institute, 10, 28,
    61–62, 73, 88
McNerney, Jim, 225–26
Malaysia, 97, 102, 108, 109, 115, 276
Malaysia Airports Holdings Berhad,
    108–9, 110
margin calls, 96
marketing, Internet-based, 60–61
Martens, Phil, 119
mature markets, 16
meetings, six-week, 242–44
mergers and acquisitions, 171–72, 175
Merrill Lynch, 92, 93
middle class:
    frugal innovation and, 75
    growth in, 7, 67–74, 83
Middle East, 5, 69, 73, 82, 144–45,
    230, 256, 271, 273–76
    sovereign wealth from, 29, 35
mining, 51, 77, 81, 82
Mitsubishi Heavy Industries, 265, 269
Mittal, Sunil, 4, 98, 132–43, 223–34
mobile communications, 26, 61, 62–63,
    105, 134–43
Moody's, 40, 94, 166
mortgages, 87, 91–92, 95, 96
Mulally, Alan, 243
multicontextuality, 183, 185–87
multinationals, 99, 289
Mumbai, 16, 71, 73, 105, 110, 133
municipal bonds, 96

nationalism, 47, 89
natural gas, 56, 272
New Zealand, 277, 293
Nigeria, 69, 146, 148, 207
Nokia Siemens, 140, 141, 179

North, 143
    average age in, 72
    conditioning to think small in,
        153–55
    consumer goods from, 69
    consumers in, 212
    in financial crisis of 2008, 37–39
    free-market principles in, 7, 8, 9–10
    future competition built by, 8–10, 14,
        48, 99, 179, 208, 241–42, 258–60
    investments in, 234
    middle class in, 69
    new strategies for, 13–14, 23–24
    oil companies in, 10
    production shift back to, 52
    psychology of, 177–82
    revenue growth in, 99
    shift of economic center from, 4–6
    short-term investments in, 36–37, 53,
        113, 172–77
    Southern investments by, 29–36
    South not known by, 208
    tension with headquarters in, 216–17
    trade surpluses and deficits in, 21
    urbanization in, 70
North-South partnerships, 258–60
Norway, 29, 272, 275
Novelis, 114, 117–20

oil, 10, 29, 56, 70, 272, 273, 275
OMV Group, 273, 274
Opie, John, 159
organizational shifts, 219–45
organizational structure, 206, 219–20
"outside in" perspective, 159–60
outsourcing, 10, 134, 156

Patel, Praful, 111
pattern recognition, 63
Paulson, Hank, 39–40
performance appraisals, 235–38
Petrochemical Industries Company
    (PIC), 164–66
petrochemicals, 80, 163, 256, 272
petroleum, 36, 80
pharmaceuticals, 86, 178, 200, 258,
    284, 292
Philippines, 127, 276, 284
political power:
    economic power and, 10–11
    financial crisis of 2008 and, 37–38
political stability, 7, 55
polyethylene, 256, 273
polyolefins, 272
polypropylene, 256, 273

Powell, Bill, 53
power plants, 236
  GMR's, 106–7, 108
Prahalad, C. K., 155–56
price-earnings ratios, 15, 35
pricing philosophy, 237, 251–52,
  292–93
private equity, 15, 29
Procter & Gamble (P&G), 75, 176–77,
  242–43
  reduction of geographic scope by,
  201, 254, 255
  Singapore headquarters of, 193, 248
property rights, 55
protectionism, 21, 45–47
  North's reluctance toward, 19
  in South, 7–10
  in United States, 7, 45
purchasing power parity, 20

Qingdao, 125, 126
quantitative easing (QE2), 32

Rao, G. M., 104–9, 112
Rao, K. V. V., 107
Rao, Narasimha, 134
regulatory agencies, U.S., 38, 39–40
Reliance Industries, 98, 139
research and development (R&D),
  56, 86, 131, 176, 200, 271, 277,
  280–83, 288, 290, 292–93
Research in Motion (RIM), 154–55
resource allocation, 233–34, 240–41
resources, 16, 21, 69–70, 75–83, 272,
  273
  natural, 29
  prices of, 26
  shifts in, 220–21
  volatile, 78
Rice, John, 228
Rio Tinto mining, 77–78
Rohm and Haas, 163–68
Rubin, Robert, 39
Russia, 10, 21, 33, 50, 121
  aviation in, 263, 264–65, 267, 269

Samsung, 53, 127, 285
Sankhe, Shirish, 73
Saudi Arabia, 10, 21, 29, 36, 158–59,
  163–64
Saudi Basic Industries Corporation
  (SABIC), 36, 158–59, 163–64
Securities and Exchange Commission
  (SEC), 93, 94
securitization, 38, 87, 94–95

Seidenberg, Ivan, 26, 168
semiconductors, 14, 298
September 11, 2001, terrorist attacks,
  91, 95
shadow banking system, 38–39
Shanghai, 71, 288, 290
short-termism, 36–37, 53, 113, 172–77
Siemens, 20, 65, 127, 135, 140, 227
Silicon Valley, 55, 66, 269
Singapore, 7, 22, 46, 102, 104, 106,
  110, 141, 239–40, 281
  export-based economy of, 49
  as financial center, 14
  P&G in, 193, 248
  sovereign wealth of, 29
  3M in, 283, 286
Singh, Manmohan, 111, 134
SingTel, 138, 141
Snecma, 264, 268
social networks, 61, 62, 190, 196,
  208–9, 301
social organization, 214–17, 220–23
sourcing, 300–302
South:
  average age in, 72
  as competitive, 14–15
  consumer goods from, 69
  cost advantages in, 12
  declining U.S. influence in, 11
  digitization and, 60
  economic ecosystem of, 16
  economic principles in, 7–10
  entrepreneurial drive in, 5
  execution and growth in, 101
  fast-changing conditions in, 236
  government support in, 8–9, 12,
  13, 15
  growth in, 4–5, 13–15, 99, 192, 295,
  297
  incorporating staff from, 206, 244,
  279–82
  investments as long-term in, 36–37,
  53, 103, 173–74
  investments in North by, 33–34
  investors in, 15, 101, 106
  knowledge of North in, 207–8
  large-scale entrepreneurs in, 99–100
  low prices from, 124
  markets in, 198–99, 212–13, 256–58
  narrowing gap between North and,
  20–22
  Northern growth in, 15–24
  Northern leadership in, 219–31
  Northern understanding of, 18–24
  opportunities seen in, 97–98

playing by different rules, 8–9, 26
psychology of, 178–82
strategies and characteristics of,
148–49
talent pool in, 222
trade surpluses and deficits in, 21
urbanization in, 70–71
South Africa, 33, 82, 97
South America, 17, 88, 268, 295
Southeast Asia, 14, 31, 268
sovereign wealth funds (SWFs), 10, 29,
35, 88
Spain, 30, 230
Speth, Ralf, 100–101
Sri Lanka, 4, 141, 143
Standard & Poor's, 40, 94, 166, 167,
192
state-owned enterprises (SOEs), 56
in China, 36, 51–54
steel, 80, 81
stock exchanges, 34–35
stock markets, 10, 15, 30, 95, 96
strategic bets, 162–72
Strauss-Kahn, Dominique, 33
surpluses, trade, 21

Taiwan, 7, 14, 22, 30, 135, 283
talent, 81–82, 84, 222, 223–30, 241,
249–50
Tata Group, 99, 139
team building, 213–14
telecom, 3–4, 85–86, 135–43, 174, 179,
188–89
Telles, Marcel Herrmann, 122
Thailand, 22, 31, 32, 88–89, 115, 276,
283
3M, 181, 225–26, 257, 260
APAC region and, 277–78, 279–93
Asian leadership in, 279–82
committing to markets ahead of
growth by, 276–79
manufacturing hubs of, 282–85
product platforms of, 285–90
tired assets, shedding of, 168–69
total shareholder return (TSR), 172–73,
175, 230
Toyota, 63, 168
trade imbalances, 21, 22, 83, 88–89
Treasury Department, U.S., 39, 95
Turkey, 33, 104, 122

unemployment, 9, 37, 73
digitization and, 64–65
in U.S., 43, 54, 96
Unilever, 69, 227, 256

Uniqlo, 34, 69
United Aviation Corporation (UAC),
264–65, 267
United Kingdom, 86, 101, 121, 127,
136, 174, 192, 290
foreign investments in, 35
trade deficit of, 21
United States, 3, 14, 21, 29, 35, 54, 71,
77, 86, 121, 123, 135, 170, 192,
200, 208, 275, 281, 286
bailouts in, 96
decline of manufacturing in, 9
declining exports from, 11
declining influence in South by, 11
economy of, 4–5, 22, 34, 92, 295
financial crisis in, 91–96
foreign investments in, 35
free market in, 45–46, 55, 93
GDP of, 47
Haier in, 128–31
housing bubble in, 87, 91–92
institutional investors in, 36
market size of, 34, 192, 263
middle class in, 69
nineteenth-century, 97
political polarization in, 47, 56
problems facing, 55–58
protectionism in, 7, 45
tech entrepreneurs in, 65–68
trade deficit with China of, 22, 29,
35, 38, 87

Vale, 14–15, 46–47, 77–78
Veiga Sicupira, Carlos Alberto da, 122
venture capitalists, 66–67
Verizon, 26, 168, 174
vertical integration, 80–81, 164
Vietnam, 17, 33, 52, 83, 85, 88–89, 276
3M in, 281, 283–84, 285, 290, 293
vision, tangible, 210–12
Vivendi, 135–36
Vodafone, 143, 174

wage differentials, 12, 19
Wall Street, 86, 93, 158, 163, 165, 230,
232
shareholder value as goal of, 9, 38–49
short-term gains preferred by, 36–37,
172–74, 175–76
Walmart, 60, 69, 121, 128–29
water, 82–83, 182
Welch, Jack, 81, 159, 225
Whitman, Meg, 176
Wipro, 10, 81
World Bank, 53–54

INDEX

World Trade Organization (WTO), 46, 77

Zain Group, 4, 34, 132, 141–42, 144–45, 210

Zhang Ruimin, 124–31
Zhu Rongji, 157
Zook, Chris, 156
Zuckerberg, Mark, 66

Ram Charan is a world-renowned business adviser, author, and speaker who has spent the past thirty-five years working with many top companies and CEOs of our time. In his work with companies such as GE, MWV, Bank of America, DuPont, Novartis, Coca-Cola, Merck, EMC, 3M, Verizon, Tata Group, Aditya Birla Group, and Grupo RBS, he is known for cutting through the complexity of running a business in today's fast-changing environment to uncover the core business problems. His real-world solutions, shared with millions through his books and articles in top business publications, have been praised for being practical, relevant, and highly actionable—the kind of advice you can use Monday morning.

Ram's introduction to business came early while working in the family shoe shop in a small town in northern India, where he was raised. He earned an engineering degree in India and soon after took a job in Australia and then in Hawaii. When his talent for business was discovered, Ram was encouraged to pursue it through formal education. He earned MBA and doctorate degrees from Harvard Business School, where he graduated with high distinction and was a Baker Scholar. He served on the faculties of Harvard Business School and Northwestern University.

Ram's work takes him around the globe nonstop and gives him an unparalleled, up-to-date insider view of how economies and leading companies operate. His timely, concrete advice is a powerful tool in navigating today's uncertain business climate. Former chairman of GE Jack Welch says that Ram "has the rare ability to distill meaningful from meaningless and transfer it in a quiet, effective way without destroying confidences," while Ivan Seidenberg, the former CEO of Verizon, calls Ram his "secret weapon."

Ram has authored or coauthored fifteen books since 1998 that have sold over 2 million copies in more than a dozen languages. *Execution,* which he coauthored with former Honeywell CEO Larry Bossidy in 2002, was a number-one *Wall Street Journal* bestseller and spent more than 150 weeks on the *Wall Street Journal* bestseller list. He also has written for many publications, including *Harvard Business Review, Fortune, Financial Times, Forbes, BusinessWeek, Time, Chief Executive,* and *USA Today.*